A LIFE IN THE DAY
OF YEVICH ROMANOV

~ a rural comedy,
being the love story of Isayevich and Nadya Romanov,
to the tune of Schubert's Trout Quintet in B Flat minor,
for guitar, mandocello, balalika, piano, and harmonica

CHRISTOPHER SPARKES
• 2025 •

Published by
Filament Publishing Ltd
14, Croydon Road, Beddington,
Croydon, Surrey CR0 4PA

www.filamentpublishing.com

A Life in the Day of Yevich Romanov
by Christopher Sparkes

ISBN 978-1-915465-87-0

The right of Christopher Sparkes to be identified as the author of this work has been asserted by him in accordance with the Designs and Copyright Act of 1988.

© Christopher Sparkes 2025

Typeset in Garamond

All rights reserved. This work is protected by international copyright and may not be copied by any means, for commercial purposes, without the prior written consent of the publishers.

Cover photograph, by Nicole Hoogenboorn
Cover Design Niamh Craigie
Inside cover: *Sun Setting Over Cornfield*
by Christopher Sparkes, 2017

WHAT PEOPLE ARE SAYING

This poem enhances the love story between two Russian scarecrows, Yevich Romanov and his wife Nadya who is expecting their first scaretit. When the gift of fatherhood comes along, Yevich becomes a scarecrow, in a different key. There are also dark moments when he ponders on the death of his brother Python. The lines are laced with comedy and clever references and conversations between the couple which are spoken in awkward English add to the charm of the piece. Like any expectant father, the scarecrow is on tenterhooks throughout Nadya's long labour, but when, finally, his son Goo-Gaga is born, he is overjoyed; it gives him a new perspective in life and he offers a prayer up for the child thing hoping that he may be a blessing and not a curse.
~ Denise Bennett

A feast of tactile rhythms and chewy language. Oracular lines of poetry flow in a vernacular speech spiced with grandeur, honouring a great resonant subject, the birth of perhaps a redeemer. Extraordinary. ~ George Marsh

Original, inventive, with linguistic somersaults taking centre stage on every page, who'd imagine a humble scarecrow being raised to such literary heights? Chris Sparkes has created a heart-felt tour de force in his *Life in the Day of Yevich Romanov*. Scaretits, hold on tight to your straw hats! ~ Maggie Sawkins

This is a love story that compels like no other: a tour de force of impressive linguistic invention and laugh-out-loud playfulness 'in the year of who-knows-when'. Sheer delight! ~ Robyn Bolam

It makes you want to weep. This is liquid gold. ~ Sarah Lucas

BY THE SAME AUTHOR

Biblical
Published by Filament

The Keys of the Kingdom Holy Bible (hardback, 2022. Out of print)
The Keys of the Kingdom Holy Bible (ebook, 2023)
The Keys of the Kingdom Holy Bible (paperback, 2023)
The Keys of the Kingdom Holy Bible (leatherette, 2024)
The Study Companion to the Keys of the Kingdom Bible (2024)
Searching For Hell (2025)

Poetry

Kissing Through Glass (Mighty Conqueror Productions, 1986)
One Word of Truth (Sons of Camus, 2011)
Counter Intelligence (www.secretpoetry.co.uk, 2015)

Academic

So You Want to Be a Writer? (with Ray Sparkes, Packard Publishing, 2004)
Grammar Without Groans (with Ray Sparkes, Packard Publishing, 2004)

TABLE OF CONTENTS

CONTENTS

	Page
Foreword, by Raymond Keene OBE	i-iii
Preface	iv-v
1. What the scarecrow did	1
2. A hard life improves the vision	7
3. Izzatreallyso?	10
4. Are angels not attending spirits?	14
5. Reception class for gallyblaggers and hodmedods	24
6. The spirit of Urbania	32
7. In mourning for life	35
8. In the Spinning Waters	46
9. This could be the last time or, One word of truth outweighs the whole world	53
10. To virtue add knowledge	57
11. Scales of Python	64
12. Nadie done baba?	77
13. Fries my wig, Roxanna	84
14. The Earth was void and without form	90
15. Wedding of the scarecrows	100
16. Putrefaction	103
17. An ezra, a bolchek, and a ruby	106
18. Trout in cling-film	111
Ephanerothee-English Glossary	114
Sky Music	117
Afterword	118
Selection of epics and long narrative poems	119-120

CAST

in order of appearance

Yevich Isayevich Romanov: Scarecrow, husband of Nadya
Nadya Nadezhda Bukharinovna Romanov of that Nik:
    Scarecrow, wife of Yevich
Jane Amanda Ellis: Maternity patient at Ephanerothee Hospital
Jessie Hypsenor: Maternity ward receptionist
Upper-Valdaskaya: Midwife
Nurse
Jen: Student
Jezza: Student
Python: Brother of Yevich
Dean JW Burgon Abodski: Farmer
Roxanna Abodski: Farmer and wife of Dean
Alexander: Brother of Yevich
Java: Brother of Yevich
Ludvig Hezekiah Romanov: Brother of Yevich
Levi (also known as 'Python'): Brother of Yevich
Goo-Gaga Abodski Romanov: Son to Yevich and Nadya
Santiago 'Jim' Vonbarden: Colleague and friend of Yevich
Muzz Amy Checker: Bureaucrat

Foreword
by Raymond Keene OBE
MA Trinity College Cambridge
International Chess Grandmaster

AN EPIC FOR OUR TIMES

Epic poetry might be considered a prehistoric art form, the stuff of long dead white authors, such as Homer, Virgil, Dante and Milton, the dread and terror of English A level students. It is no accident that much of such epic poetry takes place physically in the realms of the dead, with visitations to Hades forming key components of *The Odyssey*, *The Aeneid*, *The Divine Comedy* and, of course, *Paradise Lost*.

In his new work Christopher Sparkes seeks to revive the Epic and imbue it with the breath of modern life, much as the 19th century French poet Baudelaire exhorted pictorial artists to abandon the customary *fêtes galantes*, relegate them to the *Neiges d'antan* of Villon, and focus instead on the rich seam of potential offered by the dynamic vibrancy of modern life.

Epic narratives can come in various forms, such as Shakespeare's cycle of History plays. William Shakespeare is also, of course, an opulent source for verbal troves. He can be credited with many achievements, not least, in my opinion, with writing the key texts which actually created English national and linguistic identity.

Shakespeare's play *Henry VIII* brings to a close the mighty history cycle commencing with *Edward III*. The latter is now generally regarded as, at least partly, a Shakespeare original, and one of the very few which specifically mention chess:

"And bid the lords hold on their play at chess,
For we will walk and meditate alone."
(Scene 3 in the Royal Shakespeare Company edition.)

The cycle continues with *Richard II*, *Henry IV* Parts One and Two, *Henry V*, *Henry VI* Parts One, Two and Three, and *Richard III*. It is my opinion that this huge dramatic cycle, essentially one long play, represents the true English national epic in a way that

Beowulf (too early in our national lifeline) and *Paradise Lost* (too Latinate for most readers, though a treat for those who like their English poetry in a Latin word order) do not.

If I am correct, then the Shakespeare histories together create our epic poem of national identity, on a par with Homer's *Iliad* and *Odyssey*, Virgil's *Aeneid*, Dante's *Divine Comedy*, the Welsh *Mabinogion*, Finland's *Kalevala*, Portugal's *Lusiads* and, for the Hebrew people, the epic story of the Hebrew Bible, or Old Testament.

In the course of his plays and poetry Shakespeare deployed a vocabulary of around 35,000 words. This is a global record, apart from that Olympic level logodaedalus, James Joyce, who operated with a staggering vocabulary in *Finnegans Wake* of over 64,000 words. However, many of these were one-off inventions, never since revived and incomprehensible to the multitude, not so much caviar to the general as gibberish to almost everyone, apart from Joycean scholars ensconced in their most adamantine of ivory towers.

In practice, even the most literate of English speakers tend to operate within a maximum of 15,000 words, with the average being in the range 3,000-5,000. Enhanced vocabulary liberates thinking and creativity, equating freedom of expression with breadth of thinking and outreach of communication potential.

However, we now largely inhabit an increasingly reductive communicative environment, a hostile territory now challenged by Sparkes, who boldly rejects a largely non-verbal landscape, dominated by emojis, icons and abbreviations, with would-be aspirations to eloquence arbitrarily truncated in Tweets to a prescribed maximum of characters. One might describe it as verbal grunting, rather than efflorescence, with the full expression of cerebration now widely regarded as an evil to be avoided at best, or ignored at worst.

Fortunately, our new worshipper at the shrine of Homer and his poetic descendants represents an oasis in this wasteland. Brevity may be the soul of wit, but this does not necessarily imply that unexpurgated expression, as practised in the following pages, is anathema to our little grey cells.

A Life in the Day of Yevich Romanov is, as noted above, written by Christopher Sparkes – a fresh voice in the revival of the Epic. Sparkes has already devoted 28 years towards creating a new

English translation of the Bible. His Epic Poem is deeply imbued with classical, humanist and Christian symbolism and it pays coruscating homage to other examples of the epic form such as Milton's *Paradise Lost*. Yevich Romanov follows in the footsteps of Homer's *Odysseus*, the Anglo-Saxon *Beowulf* and other heroes of the genre, which typically create the totality of the life of a man and flesh it out with multiple new dimensions.

Epic poems famously depict the experiences of a hero, in this case Yevich Romanov, in a struggle to overcome the hostile forces that try to prevent his success, whether it be in battle, in love, in the attainment of enlightenment or remaining true to his moral principles. All of the great challenges of human existence confront Yevich Romanov, as he anticipates the arrival of his first child and ponders the meaning of human life.

As with Milton's epic poem *Paradise Lost*, there is a timeless quality to the depiction of Romanov's life in Ephanerothee. There are other parallels with Milton's stupendous creation of Satan, on the one hand a supernatural figure, on the other infused with human emotions and desires.

The character of Yevich Romanov similarly hovers between two conditions, his life as a scarecrow and his raw emotions as a man, husband and soon-to-be father. As the author tells us, his poem could be set either in a distant age or in a post-AI world that has lost or forgotten earlier technologies. But ultimately Yevich Romanov is witness to and engaged by a battle between good and evil which has already claimed the life of his brother Python, leaving him to wonder what sort of world his child will inherit.

Before the advent of literacy and the written word, arresting stories such as *A Life in the Day of Yevich Romanov* were often told in the form of poetry, which could be easily memorised. Epic poems called for prodigious feats of memory, though, and they were performed by professional story tellers, bards and actors. For this reason, perhaps, the long epic poem is a much neglected form in our age of tweets, instant information and AI-generated text. Yet we are increasingly recognising the value of deep engagement with the thoughts, knowledge and creations of other people, both from the distant past and in our present age, as demonstrated in Sparkes's creation of *A Life in the Day of Yevich Romanov*.

Preface

The time in which *A Life in the Day of Yevich Romanov* is set is floating. It's an era when people have literary knowledge. Contemporary cultural markers hint of an era having advanced and having left behind Artificial Intelligence. On the other hand, it's a deeply agrarian age. The title's "in the day of" might suggest a long-gone era.

Isayevich "Yevich" Ishi Romanov and Nadya Nadezhda Bukharinovna Romanov of that Nik are gallyblaggers, hodmedods. There is no doubt for diligent employment they stand in fields scaring off birds from the good produce of the land. The district they live in is Ephanerothee, Greek meaning "brought to light". Yevich and Nadya of that Nik are Russian made, and speak awkward English.

Yevich has character and appearance of scarecrowness, yet is perceptive, well-read, on the other hand clumsy. This is no Ovidian metamorphosis, no wolf in sheep's clothing. More a sheep in wolf's clothing, bird-scarer in man's garments, the scarecrowness of the comic tramp.

The narrative opens with Yevich, from whose point of view the story is narrated, pulling his feet out of the sod to go home and fetch his trout rod for the enjoyment of an evening's fishing on the river. At bedtime he discovers from his wife, Nadya of that Nik, that they are expecting their first child.

On a dark winter morning, as the North wind polishes the ice-filled fields, Yevich is operating his vocation in a field when he receives an urgent call from Nadya. He races home and drives her to the maternity hospital in his tractor.

During Nadya's long labour, Yevich goes to town for lunch and makes friends with two young people who perform a Shakespeare scene for him. He surveys the materialism of the urban world. In a street scene, children are feeding tame birds, but the birds see Yevich and fly away.

As Yevich has to sit long hours in the waiting room of the maternity ward, his mind runs over events of the past, especially concerning his scarecrow brothers, one of whom, Python, was a pop singer, astrologer, idle anarchist and figure of uselessness who comes to his end, knifed by drug-running gangsters. Yevich contemplates his life on the farm and various interests, his spiritual renaissance, and his first time meeting Nadya.

While the culture seems stable, there's threat in the air. The music of his murdered brother, destructive and violent, is becoming popular. It's understood by the two young people he meets in the street. Yevich cites lyrics from a Python song, and it's a concern for what sort of world he and Nadya might be bringing a child into.

The eighteen chapters, cantons, are introduced with mock prologues or arguments, in pale imitation of Milton's *Paradise Lost*. They're elliptical, and strike a different register of language. A glossary describes foreign and unusual words, a feature that Greek philosopher Aristotle describes in his book *Poetics* as an element of poetic diction.

A Life in the Day of Yevich Romanov all began around 2006 with this from Welsh poet RS Thomas:

> and there the scarecrow walked
> over the surface of the brown
> breakers, tattered like Christ. *

And there is this too from Thomas:

> Of whom
> does the scarecrow remind,
> arms wide as though pierced
> by the rain's nails? **

Christopher Sparkes, May 2025

---

* from "Farming Peter", *Later Poems*, Macmillan, 1984

** from "Come Down", *Mass for Hard Times*, Bloodaxe, 1992

"THE parish of Selborne lies in the extreme corner of the county of Hampshire, bordering on the county of Sussex, and not far from the county of Surrey; is about fifty miles south-west of London, in latitude 51, and near midway between the towns of Alton and Petersfield ... The prospect is bounded to the south-east and east by the vast range of mountains called the Sussex-downs." ~ Gilbert White, *The Natural History of Selborne*, 1789

"The human soul longs for things higher, warmer and purer than those offered by today's mass living habits, introduced as if by a calling card by the revolting inflation of commercial advertising, by TV stupor and intolerable music ... What is the joy about?"
~ *Alexander Solzhenitsyn Speaks to the West*, 1978

1. What the scarecrow did

In early spring, in the fifteenth year of the reign of the supreme monarch Razórmindd, then Enkratia and Didrachmon and Arpagenta and Eugene being noble tetrarchs of Ephanerothee, Isayevich 'Yev' Ishi Romanov has drifted off after his shift has ended; the afternoon has begun to wear away when he wakes; he squelches his boondockers out of the Earth and under a sullen sky of hooknosed woe he walks puppet-legged to Horatio Cottage for his rod and takes himself down to the Hippie Moon River & District Fly Fishery where a different kind of news runs on the wind; the river holds its surgery and he attends; you can hear the mandocello of the soundtrack.

* * *

His conker eyes give a sharp wince;
a strong clump of gust screws him
two full twists against the soil.

Several thumps of wind; an eyebrow lifts;
out of the dust of sleep the scarecrow's body
makes a single twitch. Turns from the landscape

of forgetfulness, and with a sucking sound out of
heavy clods drills his gumboots; shoots an arm out
to hold the hat down with a free hand;

he ambles across the brown soil of the field,
leaving trails of chaff. As he moves along,
the clumsy contraption of him buckles at the hip

like a theatre puppet, then hoists up again,
as if he were raised by sky-strings;
chaff blows off his clothes and flows

into the windy distance. Rooks caw around the one tree
like a flock of seagulls trailing behind a fishing boat;
it's humid; baggy clouds are hanging

on the same sky-strings, and every tree
in the valley is knocking off its head
against wild buffs of western wind,

and leaves are clapping their hands for it all.
He clambers his bad leg across a stile,
and gathers his gear from Horatio Cottage

for some liquefactious casting of a fly
for the trout saved in the flood,
silver skins as bright as the Pistol Star.

In the warm rustling rain he strolls,
like a tatty kind of nineteenth century hobo,
on the banks of the freshly-stocked Hippie Moon River,

whistling every phrase he knows from Schubert's *Trout*.
He halts at the millpool, like a great Greek thinker,
or Cicero contemplating the lofty spirit.

The water gushes in the pool, as if churned
by the Angel of the Waters in a healing bath,
and sprays of foam light up and jingle

like sixpences for the poor. Here he thinks it out,
sages, leave your contemplations,
brighter visions beam afar ...

On upstream he walks until, at a stone's heave
from the pool, he comes to his favourite bending
of the waters, and the scarecrow

from his river rod pulls out several yards
of line, ties an elk hair sedge,
hackled like a squirrel's tail,

and he whips his cane rod, and the lasso of line
curls through the drenched wind like a buzzard's cry,
and his fly of falsehood skids along the water,

like a wind-blown thistledown seed-head, to the side
of the echoing ring of a trout rise. The merry sedge sails
on the river like a fishing smack or small river craft,

the sunken bend of the hook wobbling
in the water like a rudder. Two more tries
and the brown trout slashes at the sedge fly;

there's a crack inside the scarecrow's head
and, for the trout, the delicious sedge fly is, after all,
only a single-masted phantom ghost ship,

the barb of the hook a deathly gangplank.
The fish draws the line underneath the boil
of water and down into the weedbeds.

The scarecrow lets the fish head back downwards
then lifts his rod, and the line plucks
with the tautness created by the powerful back muscle

of the trout. The scarecrow's heart so hammers
in his chest that his waistcoat buttons burst,
and the stuffing leaks out of his chest, popping like bubble-wrap.

He scoops the fat and flapping fish
into his net, and admires his majestic trout
in its coat of sequins and golden underside

painted like the Moon washing its blonde long hair
in the river; he clangs the thing goodnight, goodnight, farewell,
shovels the straw back inside his shirt,

closes the iron swing-gate behind him,
and hurries up the puddled farm track,
his rod slung on his shoulder like a rifle.

The scarecrow's recovered chest puffs out
with the jaunty air of a man happy in the late evening rain,
the honk of cowdung from another farm

whizzing in his nose. The trout slides around
in one of his slimy pockets, and as the scarecrow man walks
he rings out in his reedy voice

his favourite guitar and blues harmonica cantatas,
and the net clipped to the scarecrow's belt
taps against his hip like a tambourine,

and all through the thrash of rain sticks
he is occupied in thinking to himself
in A-flat major, give or take a gap

between the teeth, and he sings:
The great bear's bloody paw is raised:
the noble character disdains;

the dragon's red-hot innards burn:
the great bear rumbles in its chains.
By mercy will the world be saved,

with twanging strings and magic flutes,
for poets and exiled scarecrow men,
with shaven heads and clumsy boots ...

All inside Horatio Cottage rests quiet.
He puts the fish guts in a bag, and that bag
in another bag, and ties it up and rams the lot

down the side of the green council bin.
He cooks his trout with spices on an oiled baking tray,
and eats it with its skin still on like bacofoil.

When he goes up to bed, his wife, the beauty star
Nadya Nadezhda Bukharinovna Romanov of that Nik, her breasts
heavy as Kerry's under her silk imported gown from Russia,

comes into the bedroom holding up to the light
a glass tube he hadn't seen before.
She looks into his large crayon'd eyes

and she draws a speech bubble out of her face
and it's saying to her husband, 'Well well, Mister Scarecrow,
who's going to be a daddy then?'

✽

2. A hard life improves the vision

Yev Romanov, deep-browed on the chessboard floor of the ploughed fields of Saddleback Farm; in work a stillness beyond understanding; all whingeing is dungforked.

* * *

Somewhere beyond the Saddleback Hills
in the fields of Saddleback Organic Farm
a clumsy contraption without genealogy stands.

His arms extend outwards,
as if an umpire were admonishing a bowler
that he's delivered wide of the mark.

Pale rags drape off his limbs.
When the wind blows
the tatters lift
and an arm beckons
and waves to no one
and to everyone.

Season presses into season,
the harvest falls,
winter bites like a viper's tooth,
the savage sun-slash of the summer,
year after revolving year

the interminable nothingness of thought,
the thought of interminable nothingness,
the scarecrowness of being,
an obsession of not being
and yet of being,
a clumsy contraption
with a fixed gaze,
like a neural paralysis
of the nineteenth, twentieth, twenty-first,
twenty-second, twenty-third centuries.

So many hours, so many days,
so many weeks
of solitude
when splitting winds
bend arthritic knees of groaning trees,
or a tropic Sun beats
dragon breath
on summer's king
but, for compensation,
there lies the ecstasy of the stretching vista
of the hills,
the strength of health
against the hardships of Earth's ice and fire,
the fixedness, durability
to perform that which is menial
which those of discontented centre
and disruptive nature
are unable or unwilling to perform.

Conker eyes
moisten in the wind,
a fly crawls up the arm,
a strong gust blows his billycock sky piece,
turns him on his stake of Christ,
and you could swear to
suspecting a muscular impulse,
the twitch at the farmer's touch
when he renews the coat
and drives the upright
hard into the soil.

The saviour of all men's appetites,
a man of sorrows
on the hill of hills,
he loves the birds
for the beauty of their flight
and their elaborate pantomime of feathers;
his employment, though,
is to terrify them shitless.

3. Izzatreallyso?

In the first days of the first month, in the sixteenth year of the reign of virtuous King Razórmindd, out in the boondocks in a field of Saddleback Farm, an unholy mass of birds on the wrong wing, a bunch of stiffs. Through the starbeating night, the man of wood has hornswoggled bony time out of another night of life-engendering labour; nearly gets his head electrocuted when his gadget goes off and his Zygo's ready for the next generation and the information is stored in the light itself and everything in the Universe is still except for the Zygo's child and Yevich Romanov is off in a cloud of gas and dust, and the angel seems to be leading the horse that way and the birds couldn't give a flying bagpipe ...

* * *

In the year of who-knows-when,
while a few late stars of washed gold
like the steel rivets on denim jeans
were still crackling over Saddleback Organic Farm,
a flock of Homeric rooks
shot with adrenalin,
as if they'd been horridly startled,
all at once lifted themselves
off the cold ground
like rising stars of darkness.

The scarecrow hadn't noticed
those naughty birds behind him
in a crafty corner of the field
of beet. For a living moment
he'd been busy thinking along,
away from the existential void,
thinking along on his elegy to rooks:
Big black flappy rooks,
big black crappy flooks.

His soul twitches at the sight of scavengers.
The sky was charcoaled
in galloping darkness and those birds
should have been asleep in trees.
Automated by his own triumph of the will,
Yevich swivelled on the axis of his pole
and cupped his hands into a megaphone
and yelled at them in his fiercest voice, '*Shoo, shoo!*'
and waved his arms like an angry puppet.

It was a sound as loud as clanging
of a fire station bell that had shaken
the birds just now. They couldn't bear the noise
of it. Then they heard talking,
a ghostly voice somewhere near their trees.
The scarecrow took off his gloves
and flipped open the source
of the noisy disturbance – the number of Nadya.
He covered a straw hand over his cold ear.

'Hello, my love, my last lovely Romanov of that Nik ...'
'Yevich, Yevich,' she interrupted him,
'think waters breaking! Contractions.
Little boy blue on way.'
'Izzatso, izzatso?' the rooks heard from the scarecrow.

Yevich snapped his smartphone shut
and belted back to Horatio Cottage,
shouting 'Jingle-jangle day to ya all!'
and leaping with such a coordination
as if being chased in a Punch and Judy show,
taking care to tread lightly as he could
over the kind beet-bearing earth
in the dark and icy air
of his final watch before the dawn.

The gang of rooks dropped from low branches,
scraps of black silk parachutes,
and settled themselves down again
to scoffing at the beet seed. Other rooks
leaned forward on the branch
of a Biblical tree, waiting, their heads turned.
'Caw, caw, man of straw!' squawked the rooks.
'Bottle the smart talk!' the scarecrow
shouted back from the gate post.
'Gang of dirty rattlesnakes! Rat-hawks!'

He knew the farmer wouldn't trouble him:
cut short but conscientiously fulfilled

was his long night-shift of frightening
birds and foxes and sweetcorn-nibbling badgers
and wolves away from the field.

He pressed his hands in the small of his back
and stretched himself, feeling the ache
of boiler wood, and he was away
– away to see through the final moments
of a thing incredible, the birthing
of his firstborn into the rural landscape –
and shaking it back to Horatio Cottage.
When he reached the stile he stopped
and shouted at the birds,
'Now you skunk-beards, leave
beet seeds *alone*! *And* jackdaws.
All just watch it. Black bolts of plague!
Forked lightning! Bats and dragons
hiding in bushes. Ghosts in
undergloom of ivy. *Whaaaa*! *Whaaaa*!'

4. Are angels not attending spirits?

At Horatio Cottage, home of the Romanovs, a quartet for the end of time; Yevich hopes she won't be barfing. For him she has transcendental medication. A mob of underclass, Python and the Stiffs, bitter and untalented, spike the Zeitgeist; Nadya teaches stars to shine with brightness all these blonde long years, like Anaxagoras finding that the light of the Moon is not reflected from the Sun; Yevich displays the knightliness of his race; is a zoid in the cow shed; in the alektorophonia and cold-throated howl of early morning they burn jet fuel from the old 97 on the autobahn and the air is coughing.

* * *

The kitchen filled with the aroma
of lobster soup Nadya was simmering
on the stove for her husband's breakfast.
The *Époustouflante* electric fan heater,
the *generador del aire caliente*, blew
a heart-warming storm, gas-mark 100.
Yevich hurried in to find Nadya leaning
with her palms against a work surface.
She took long and slow
and deep deliberate breaths
through her conker nose. Yevich looked at her
as if she were transfigured.

Blu-tacked on the cupboard doors
were proverbs on old greetings cards
Yevich had hand-decorated
and mounted for her birthday:
'he who emptieth the kettle filleth the jug'
(that, Nadya said, was ambiguous),
and 'make sun while hay shine'.
And, in her writing: *pro yednu kveah tinu slunkah nesuitee.*

'Ah! Yev, Yev ... my dear ... Yev!'
She panted when she realized he was there.
'Your Bovril and glucosamine and linseed ...'
Yevich said, 'Hot fish n' chips n' seagulls! Look at woo!'
She said, 'Baba scarecrow soon, Yev. Yevi papa man.'
He said, 'Nadie mama woman.'
She said, 'Baba ... but how long night go, Yev?'
'Ah! Nadie,' he said. 'Long night,
freezing joints. Sometimes, Nadie,
that Druid wind not give a toss.
One day Yevich mildew ergot poison.'
Nadya asked, 'How long take Yev warming up
after ordeal of winter, Yev?'
He said, 'Four months, four months.'
She said, 'And that moonlight wolf music
you have to listen to all night.
All those conversations in the head.'
'Ah, but Nadie,' he said, 'every dawn
in summer Yev hear green prehistoric song
of early birds like symphony.'

The scarecrowman poured his wife
a glass of prune juice
and warmed his hands around the Bovril cup
then hovered them over the steam
rising from the lobster soup.
She began to say, 'Rain in Australia, Yev ...'
and Yevich put his cup down and said,
'Oh, oh, of course, Ashes, Nadie ...'
She said, 'No play in Ashes, Yev. Rain.
Drink Bovril, Yev.' Yevich slurped
his lobster soup, washed his bowl and spoon,
then began to gather Nadie's night bag:
a tape player, her favourite Beethoven *Pastoral*,
a Joan Baez recording she'd asked him
to make in preparation,
and the *Louange* movements
of the Messiaen *Quartet for the End of Time*,
and slipped some Bach in too.
He helped her with a softly-belted coat
on top of her maternity frock,
as they stood framed together
in the darkness of the kitchen window.

Nadya tied her belt, hung a pan up,
and turned to her husband saying,
'Python's rowdy disharmonious song
on radio again, Yev. Bad music, bad.
Bad new ideas. Creeping in stealth now.'
Yevich began to ask which song they played

but she anticipated him and said,
'You know, Yev, Bubonic thug stuff:
> *Yuh enemies uv new*
> *it a new generation*
> *yuh enemies uv new*
> *yah yah gonna f-f-f-fade out*
> *yah old generation gonna f-f-die*

That one, Yev. Of all days, Yev, of all days.'
Yevich winced and said, 'No Nadie, of all days
this is day we make bad worse for Python people!
That music, Yev call wolf music, Nadie,
not sounds of night in farm.'
She yelled, 'Ya-oooowl!' Yevich rushed
to her side saying, 'Nadie, Nadie!
Woo all right? What ...?' She pulled straw
off his jacket and let it drop to the floor
and said, 'Yeah yeah, Yev.
Ya-oooowl is howl of Wolf Music.
That Python got cachexia of mind, Yev.'

Yevich looked at Nadya's lovely bump,
then down at the piano stool, and said,
'Nadie soon honky-tonk again on tinkle-tonk.'
She said, 'Mozart good for baba brain, Yev,'
and looked in the mirror
that hung in the hall, and she dabbed
some lipstick and moved her face close
to the glass to check herself.
The hallway smelled of muddy boots

and straw and chickens. Yevich dragged
a broom over the chaff-strewn floor,
clicked off the *Époustouflante*,
hustled a chicken out of the hallway
and clamped the door of Horatio Cottage.

He held Nadya's wooden arm
as they trod along the iced-over garden path,
two tired angels shuffling down the holy road
on the last day of the world,
the flame of a torch blazing at their feet.

Nadya halted in the dark morning
and pointed to a frost-covered patch of soil.
The ice cracked its arthritic knuckles.
Nadya said, 'Montbretia in August –
thousand jewels of blood and fire.'
There was a high-pitched age of silence
as they stood, without speech,
their gaze fixed on ice-white soil,
the bulge in her coat
from her stomach holding a new generation.
She said, 'Baba play in garden.'
He said, 'Soil frosted like snowglare now.'
He looked up at the window
of the nursery room. A knot tightened
in the wood of his throat.

She held onto the gate post

and Yevich told her to take the torch
and walk cautiously to the top
of the farmyard track
while he backed the tractor out
because that would be easier
on the bump of her magnificent condition
than riding along that stony lane
on a tractor seat.
'Better for suspension, then?' she said.
He said, 'Yes, yours,'
and with their arms looped around
each other's necks he kissed her radish lips
in the fading moonlight.
Yevich had to lean himself forward
to avoid pressing on her bump.

He watched her walk away
until the only thing he could see was the light
of her torch flicker
between hedgerows along the path.

Somewhere far-off in the hills
a sheep bleated.
In Yevich's haste through the cow shed,
he tore his right thumb
on a sheet of corrugated iron
and the dark blood rippled down
from the badge of his wound
as when Lydia of Thyatira poured

her purple dyes in bowls
to sell in the market place
to the dress and garment makers of the city.
The anger of two bombs blew up inside him.
He shouted 'Faffin' sheet!'
and cursed and kicked the iron
with his boot and it buckled
against the strength of his kicking curse.
He made a tight knot with a pocket handkerchief
to stem the blood:
that would have to do for now;
he pulled a glove over the hand
in the hope Nadya wouldn't notice.

As he pressed on the accelerator
of the old 97, its horsepower smoked
and snorted, and he hurtled the loud-throbbing engine
out of the barn as though an archer god
had blazed an arrow
through the heavens across the valley.

The blue tractor clattered up the track
like the chariot of Solomon
on his way to find the Matriarch of Gallyblaggers,
as Nadya's husband's heart raced like a comet
to his beauty star,
and the tractor bounced along,
its giant wheels spitting flints
like sparks from a hoof,

and a stone chimed against the claw bar
of a sunken rusting thresher
that lay dying in the cold,
and Yevich rode his chariot
through the overgrowth of stinging nettles
beside the old cartwheel
with ivy twisting round its splintered spokes,
underneath a roll of barbed wire
and a shattered pallet.

At the top of the farm track
by the signposts at the crossroads,
Nadya Nadezhda Bukharinovna Romanov of that Nik
was standing like a Thomas Hardy figure
on that bitter, black February morning,
under the low and fading stars,
a solitary figure in a long coat,
her heaving breath clouding in front of her,
pale as a sheet in the icy stillness,
a hand pressed against her stomach.

The tractor headlights broke through
the mist of darkness in the lane.

Yevich gave an arm to his wife
and helped her step up to the footplate
and padded seat in the tractor cab.
She settled herself, and he said, 'Right, Nadie ...'
'Hold it, Yev,' said Nadya

and leaned towards his shoulder
and said, 'Yev – *ya s'tabóy
dva bérega oo adnóy rekí.*'

So the bedraggled scarecrow man
and his bedraggled scarecrow woman
rode away over the hills,
as if to some strange Bethlehem.
The scarecrow man swivelled his head
at every flying bird
and fixed them with the blank nothingness
of the scarecrow gaze until his wife
shook him at his wooden elbow
to mind the road.

Just once on the journey to the hospital,
alongside the clump of trees
where the buzzards nest,
Yevich failed to see a pothole in the road
and Nadya yelled a woodpecker yaffle,
but otherwise he steered
as if he were the most tender wheelsman
who was transporting a frail queen
to the funeral of her husband king,
and the tractor (with old canes
poking out of the back of the cab)
held the road like an ancient longboat
ploughing the sea with a team of rowers
with long and polished oars.

He said, 'Yev going to have to rise to it, Nadie.'
Nadya hummed away beside him,
pressing in her hand
the scan image of her scaretit.
To keep her entertained
Yevich spoke to her about the rooks,
how he warned them yesterday afternoon
that if they didn't keep away
he'd slay them like the Canaanites
or Assyrians, or Hector,
and he'd tie their dead bodies behind the tractor
and drag them all the way round the farm.

She said, 'Remember feed Ollie?'
'Yes, Nadie,' he said, 'fed the goat.'

'Yev, you know in *Oak and the Calf*
when he's talking about leaving Moscow
escorted by eight Geebees
and it was like an arrest in reverse
and the aeroplane took off
and he crossed himself and bowed to Russia,
well what does he mean
when he says "the Geebees goggled"?'

5. Reception class for gallyblaggers and hodmedods

At the reception desk of Ephanerothee Hospital for Men and Women of Straw Ampersand Others; lift up your heads, oh you eonian gates; and who may enter by the eonian gates? He who has clean hands and a pure heart; concerning titles and onomastics; receptor beeping signals on the screen for chief wire-puller Hypsenor, squeezing out her computer's brainworks like toothpaste, slow as a thoroughbred Stewball.

* * *

Yevich and the beautiful Nadya squeezed their way
through the hospital door
and rubbed their straw and twig-fingered hands
in the pump-action anti-septic handwash.
The maternity ward reception desk was laid out
with an untidy clutter of reception desk stuff.

Reporting herself into maternity
was a slim auburn-strawed scarecrow with a bump
bigger than her whole body.
She said in a sharp voice,
'Mrs Pitchfork, 8 The Village Street, Epha ...'
The receptionist woman interrupted:
'It's your *name* I need please, Mrs Pitchfork.'
The slim auburn woman repeated,
'I *said*, Mrs Pitchfork. You said it yourself.'

'No, no,' insisted the receptionist, 'your *name*.
What's on your birth certificate?
That's your *name*. 'Mrs' isn't a *name*.
It's a *title*, a form of address others use
when they want to address you.
You don't use it for yourself.
They used to do that back in the Vulgar Eon,
the subnographs, they did it.
You don't give yourself titles.
It common. Vulgar, Mrs Pitchfork.
They should have told you that at school.
But you have a very fine surname.'
The slim auburn-strawed scarecrow with the bump
who said part of her name was 'Mrs'
gaped at Yevich and Nadya Romanov,
as if she'd just been told she didn't look pregnant
and would not be admitted
and would she please leave.
'The lady *right*, Mrs Pitchfork,' Yevich told her.
'Mrs Pitchfork not your name. Un-hypnographic
to title you *you*.' The woman said,
'What then, Mister ...?
Are you calling me a subnograph? I ...'
'No no, just saying,' Yevich said.
'Vulgar to title *you*. Vulgar since days of Mashiachian's
Straightening Out and Excellence Restoration'
– the receptionist was nodding – 'under
the Great OQ Jangleson-Do'cker-Nottáge Administratioun.
Having twins, Mrs Pitchfork? ...

Romanov. Isayevich Romanov.'
He held out a hand.
The woman looked at his twig fingers
and turned to the receptionist
and said, 'I haven't got time for this.
I'm having twin scaretits, if you didn't know.
All *right* then! Ginger Pitchfork. *Missis.*'
The receptionist thanked her
and found her name on her screen
and handed her a badge and paperwork
to take up to the labour ward. As she turned
to go Mrs Pitchfork looked at Nadya
and said, 'More water glideth by the mill
than wots the miller of.'
And off she walked, using
her bones like a canoe paddle.

Ginger Pitchfork had gone
but the maternity ward reception nurse
wasn't looking. Nadya said to Yevich,
'*Elle est narquoise*, Yev.'
Yevich, as if he were talking to a superior,
took off his hat and said to the important woman
in his reedy voice, 'We're bedraggled people, scarecrows ...
Friends to the Martyr ... having baba.'
She looked at Nadya, then Yevich,
and frowned at them so that they weren't sure
which element she was disbelieving
and said, 'What do you hippie types

know anything about anyway?'
The woman looked down at her papers again.
Yevich put his hand on Nadya's back.
He had her two bags on his shoulder
and he stood by her side
as if he were her spear carrier.
Nadya twiddled the stamen
of a plastic flower that stuck out
of a vase on the tidy counter top.

Yevich said to the reception woman,
'Is this Counter Intelligence?' and laughed.
'Can you tell difference between rook and crow?'
Nadya prodded him. 'Don't, Yev.'
All in her own time, the reception nurse,
with a badge proclaiming her as Jessie Hypsenor,
fierce as a ruler of doom, looked aside
from her government bureaucracy forms
and boxes and duplicates and in-trays
to fidget with her mobile phone
and check her personal diary,
such a combination of bureaucracy and leisure
being more hastily to be completed
than the registration of mothers in their debut labour.

At last the waspish woman spoke:
'Sorry now. As William Shakespeare said,
"Patience is for poltroons".'
Nadya said, 'Yes, and *we're* patients.'

Yevich gave Nadya a pat of congratulation
for her quickness of wit. Tapping a pencil tip
on her teeth, Muzz Hypsenor tried out a smile
and said, '*King Henry the Sixth Part Three*.
Everybody knows that these days,
since Razórmindd, I mean. Um-um ...
What did you say the surname was?'
'Romanov. Nadya Nadezhda Bukharinovna Romanov
of that Nik.'
Yevich said, 'And Isayevich Ishi Romanov,
Horatio Cottage, Wenham, West ...'
– the receptionist's smile creased her face
but it had lost its meaning.
She interrupted, 'We only register the mothers, Sir.'
Yevich said, 'Patients for poltroons, then.'

Yevich looked at Nadya's swell
and her ravishing ankles
and he gazed on the beauty of her face.
He pulled straw and grass off his elbow
and shuffled them in a pocket
and whispered to Nadya, '*Ya s'tabóy
dva bérega oo adnóy rekí.*'
The nurse said, 'What was that?'
Nadya answered her: 'You and I
are the two banks of one river.'
Muzz Hypsenor said, 'Oh, that's sweet.'
Nadya said, 'It a joke. Russian cliché.'
'Oh,' said Muzz again. 'Can't seem to find ...'

Yevich said, 'Maybe *Scarecrow*? We're Russian
scarecrows. That's *s-k-a-i-r-g-h-c-r-e-a-u-x*.
We not extra-terrestrials: we work on
the land. We're terrestrial extras.
Nadya hypnograph, of that Nik.
Nadezhda Bukharinovna Romanov of that Nik.'
The nurse examined their appearance
with some hint of disgust,
bearing an expression suggesting
'Yeah, an' it'll be snowmen next,'
but humbled herself enough
to say, 'All right then,'
and typed in 'Nadya Scarecrow,'
then exclaimed, 'Ah yes, here we are,
Scarecrow. Horatio Cottage?'
Nadya said, 'Yeah yeah, near Saddleback Hills.'
The nurse tried to appear neither defeated
nor surprised, and she asked,
'Can you confirm your date of birth,
Mrs Romanov of that Nik?'
Nadya gave Jessie Hypsenor some approximations
for the sake of her bureaucracy,
then, still twiddling the flower, said,
'In car park no apostrophe on "visitors".
Should be like this ...'

Two nurses fixed Nadya up in a bed
and Yevich plugged Joan Baez in,
then he went off to the wazzmaráda

for a whizz and it came out yellow
because of his vitamin B regime.
Nadya reckoned it helped Yevich's circulation
in the fields on frozen winter mornings.
While he was in the wazzmaráda
he brushed his sticks and straw,
bent down on his knees and pleaded,
'Oh God, Rocka Vages ... Help ... help my pretty Nadie.'

To see Nadya gasp in pain he couldn't bear.
Her agonies were without remission
for most of the morning. He held her hand
and looked into her eyes saying,
'Nadya Nadezhda Bukharinovna look so beautiful.
Never seen look so beautiful.
You high hypnograph. You Nadya *Romanov.*'
He loved her and pitied her
and admired her and wanted her.
Nadya rolled on her side in agony,
but the midwife, Upper Valdaskaya,
with a face like a pug dog in sunglasses,
seemed more busy in other rooms
and next door sounded like a torture chamber
in an opera, and in Nadya's ears
the screams of other deliveries
were like a mega howler rocket.
She turned Joan Baez louder
and sent her husband out for lunch
and he kissed her more goodbyes

than there are stars above dark hillsides
and he picked up strands of trailing chaff
near the reception desk
and he went off to wang another parking ticket
on the tractor.

6. The spirit of Urbania

The shopping centre of Ephanerothee. If it's manufacturable (*manu* + *facere*), you might as well manufacture it; if it's saleable, you might as well sell it; if it's purchasable, you might as well purchase it; then take it back when it's gunk.

* * *

After two red-hot curries, an organic salad,
custard tart and a drink of crushed herbs
in Paradiso's in North Street,
Yevich paid his bill and shuffled out.
For a moment, outside the shop,
as if surrounded by a swarm of bees,
he went blank at the sight of crowds,
as blank as his most rigid scarecrow glare,
a paralysis of spirit. He hunched himself
in his wolfskin coat and set off
along the shopfronts in West Street,
chewing as he went on bitter apricot kernels
Nadya bought in half kilo bags
for their powerful anti-carcinogenic B17.

A silver wind hurled along the street
like a 2000 Guineas racehorse,
but Yevich was just thinking along,
thinking about thinking

and thinking about what he was thinking,
looking in windows at all that people believe
they have to have right now to transfigure themselves
into the people they want to be and the people
they're made to feel they need to be,
to fill the hole left
by the failure to purchase new lampshades,
new curtains, new shoes, new shirts, new televisions,
new CDs, new DVDs, new MP3s, new PCs, new Ipods,
new gadgets with gimmicks, new cameras,
new phones, more new phones, new novels,
new lighters, new cars, new clocks,
new watches, new holidays and new pots
new maquillage and new mugs
and new suits and newspapers and new everything.
Mugs. What *was* the joy about?
Where were they heading, these kings
and queens of Urbania, adapting the world
to themselves, with their whirlpool of pleasures
and nagging sadness of the heart,
mesmerized into all unfeeling
by the miasma of mass produce?
Their decrepit chieftains and pseudo intellectuals
have nerve-jammed them against
the dynamic triumph of the individual,
taught them they can leap out
of the confines of their skin.
If spiritual satisfaction is not able to be bought
but earned only by self-limitation,

then with the international invasion of superficial news
and information and throwaway dark glasses,
would the spirit not only wither?
Somewhere along the way, they'd leaned over
the ship of folly and dropped the key
of self-restraint on the ocean floor
where the key will tarnish
like all their trash.

The bedraggled man of the fields
feigned to look around
and smothered his mouth
and muttered to himself:
'Can't join in. I not the same.
Yev look within.
But people clever than me.
Yev not know them.
Might have shovelful of love.
Bucketful of good. Don't know.
Can't know what people carrying.'

7. In mourning for life

A seagull, sparrows and pigeons. On a bench in Ephanerothee; thumping of music from shops like the clamour of a Comanche betting ring, or a horse-shoeing down at Fort Laramie; combat between Urbania and the world of Yevich; combat against the cosmic rulers, the κοσμοκράτορες, the *kosmokratores*; Yevich and a young couple exchange light; they find him refreshing as a Glühwein station.

* * *

Yevich turned off South Star Avenue
into Dexios Street. At the side of a fish and chip van
three young children with their mother
were throwing chips on the pavement
to attract pigeons and starlings
and brave sparrows
and the children shrieked with laughter
as the ungentlemanly and unladylike birds
raced for the chips. A seagull came down
and bullied the other birds and snatched
a chip out of a pigeon's mouth
and Yevich chuckled to see the children chuckle
and he thought of his scaretit embryo
and hastened his step to join the fun.
The seagull was making another swoop down
and the children were shouting
with excitement and delight,

but the gull changed its mind,
as if jerked back up by wires
and it flew off and the sparrows and pigeons
went scattering off, in a berserk panic.
The children looked around
to see what had suddenly terrified the birds.
Yevich put a hand on his head
and said, 'Must ... must've been me. I'm a ....
Birds ... birds don't like ...'
A child shouted, 'Mummy, mummy!
It's the scarecrow man who lives
in our fields. Look, look!'
Yevich hastened off and didn't hear
the mother's answer.
Anyway, he'd been holding in for a minute or two
some long and thunderous farting.
Now he was out of earshot it could express itself
and his embarrassment turned to a trumpet of rejoicing
and a fog of lower halitosis
and he gave a long healthy aaaargh
and the wet gas stuck on his trousers
until the sharp air wiped it off
and the illumination of the atmosphere was recovered.
He imagined the children, if they'd heard,
saying his crackerjack had frightened the birds.
Just a bit of backfire, he'd say,
just a bit of friendly healthy farmyard backfire guff-a-guff.
He wondered about taking his child to Birdworld.

In his gazing at the clamorous window displays,
the scarecrow man slowed
to an amble. Forty yards up North Street
were back-to-back benches,
so he brisked his pace again and seated himself
on the outward-facing bench.
Cheerful sparrows chattered from the roofs
like small-minded intellectuals.
Yevich rubbed his bowed-down forehead in his hands.
Where does a bedraggled man's child fit
into this headlong racing orbit?
So many people in the world, rushing,
laden with bursting bags. Do they realize
their dependency on the earthworm
and the bedraggled men of the land?
For what are they mortgaging their conscience?

A young couple, all got up in black
and eating chips, came to
the benches. Yevich shuffled along
to make room. One said, 'Thanks, man,'
and Yevich said hello and grinned
and retreated back into himself.
Each time the female reached her fingers
in her chip bag, her jacket sleeve was revealing
a length of decorative script
that Yevich was unable to decipher.
He almost had the nerve to ask,
then the male leaned over the female's lap

and handed his bag of chips towards Yevich.
'Fancy a chip, mate?'
Yevich took one and thanked him
and the male character said, 'No man, have the lot.
I can't eat.' Yevich took the steaming chips,
chuckled, and said, 'Had lunches at Paradiso already!'
and the couple laughed with him.

Now he could take the opportunity to ask
about the writing on the young woman's forearm.
'Writing on sleeve? Can't read it.'
The girl made a shudder against the cold.
She lifted her sleeve and said, 'Oh that?
It says *covered in woe*. Look.
The other sleeve says *save our souls*.
Jezza's got the same, ain't you, Jezza?'
Yevich could see it now, yes, *covered in woe ... save our souls*.
He blew on a handful of chips
and said, '*Why*? And *who* you asking?'
and stuffed three chips in.
'We're in mourning for life,' the girl said.
'It's doing a number on my head.
Like, you know, what's-er-name in Chekhov. Masha.'
Yevich said, 'Chekhov? Oh. *We're* Ru ...'
The girl said, 'Yeah, did it in A-level,
din't we, Jezza? These chips are good.
Go on Jezza, eat some.'
'Yeah, Soph, it was Masha,' said the male,
rolling up his left sleeve. 'An' I've got this

on my arm. Look. *RIP my life.*
Don't know *who* we're asking, man.
Don't know. Never thought about that.
'Ave *you*, Soph? Anybody out there, I s'pose.'

The girl Soph said, 'We're doing *Henry the Sixth.*
You want to hear it, man? Come on, Jezza.'
She stood, and pulled her friend up by the hand.

SOPH: What is it but to make thy sepulchre
And creep into it far before thy time?
JEZZA: The sands are numbered that make up my life.
SOPH: Would I were dead, if God's good will were so!
For what is in this world but grief and woe?
O God! methinks it were a happy life
To be no better than a homely swain;
To sit upon a hill, as I do now,
To carve out dials quaintly, point by point,
Thereby to see the minutes how they run,
How many makes the hour full complete,
How many hours brings about the day,
How many days will finish up the year,
How many years a mortal man may live.
JEZZA: Here burned my candle out; ay, here it dies.
SOPH: Cold biting winter mars our hoped-for hay.
JEZZA: My sick heart shows
That I must yield my body to the earth
And, by my fall, the conquest to my foe.
Thus yields the cedar to the axe's edge,

Whose arms gave shelter to the princely eagle,
Under whose shade the ramping lion slept,
Whose top-branch overpeer'd Jove's spreading tree
And kept low shrubs from winter's powerful wind.
These eyes, that now are dimmed with death's black veil,
Have been as piercing as the mid-day sun
To search the secret treasons of the world;
The wrinkles in my brows, now filled with blood ...
SOPH: And live we how we can, yet die we must.

'Hooray, hooray!' The bedraggled man was standing
and shouting and banging his hands.
He seated himself back down
and said, 'You're good, good!
Still got cheer in you two, then?'
Soph said, 'Well, those are our favourite lines.
Do you want to hear some more?'
Yevich said, 'Henry? Ummm ...
No, no. All about death. Choose *life*.'
Jezza said, 'You're a strange one then, aren't you, man?'
Yevich rushed a chip down his throat
and answered, 'Ha-ha! Yevich Romanov. Yev.
We're Russian. You heard of Python Romanov?
Brother. My brother.' 'Nah!' said Jezza.
'You ... you Python's brother? *Really*, man?'

The young couple were much impressed
they'd unwittingly found themselves
in the company of a relative of Python.

Yevich related to them the day
when Python attempted to knock his brains out
with an axe
and how crazy Python lived
and the unpublished circumstances
leading to his death.
Yevich said, 'Python mind-poisoning serpent.
Worst of subnographs. Controlled by goombahs.
Like snake in lavatory pipes. Wanted subvert
and smash. Only solution – smash *their* works.
Only understand fist. Crush kingdom like custard powder.
Like Bubonic plague, whole country crumbling
under Python's goombahs. Mourning of good mind.
Python was brother but *not* brother.
Python assassinator of good mind.
Now listen, Python sang *we gonna f-f-f-fade out*,
but today great – Yev wife having baba!
But you too young for grief. Ask Rocka Vages.
Big Kosmokrator. Helped *me*.'

The man of the land took a small book
from his pocket and opened it at the place
where a blade of straw
and a card were tucked
and from the card he read slowly
in his Russian accent:
'Rescue me from blood-guiltiness, oh Elohim,
You, Elohim of my salvation,
and my tongue will sing aloud

of Your righteousness.
Oh Yahweh, open my lips
and my mouth will show Your praise,
for You do not desire sacrifice,
otherwise I would give it.
You do not delight in burnt offering.
The great sacrifice of Elohim *is* a broken spirit;
a broken and a contrite heart,
oh Elohim, You will not despise.'

'Beautiful, beautiful,' the young couple said,
and 'Ah, that's beautiful, beautiful, man,' Jezza said.
Yevich said, 'Think it from Gospa Ize-hiyah,
or Book of Palms. Card not say.'
Jezza said, 'That's the sort of stuff
you get on all these medieval scripted cards
we keep seeing. Never bother looking at them really.'
Yevich said, 'Jim gave me at farm.'
Soph said, 'You got blood then, Mr Scarecrow Man?'
and, 'That thing you read,
it started about "blood-guiltiness".'
The scarecrow man laughed and said,
'Don't know. Got *some*thing!'

Jezza asked, 'What do you *do* then, man,
like for living out the semi-fiction of our lives?'
Yevich answered, 'Scare birds.
Work organic farm, bailiff trout river. Cosmic jobs.'
Jezza said, 'Stakhanovite energy, man!'

Soph said, 'Oh cool, cool! As the great man said,
"Only those who decline to scramble up
the career ladder are interesting as human beings.
Nothing is more boring than a man with a career."
Alexander Solzhenitsyn. *Gulag Archipelago Volume 3*, 1978.
How can we be expected to malform ourselves
into the shapes demanded by standardized political
and industrial well-being, and only exist
as *technically* alive, like we're somebody's cabbages
on drip feeds? We're not *doing* it, Mr Romanov.'
Yevich said, 'You two fine people ... Ah! *Time*!
Must get bodging, go see Nadie.
Baba Romanov soon. Birth like rebirth Romanov.
Yev tired, could do with ...'
Soph said, 'The drowsy syrup of an afternoon's sleep.'
Yev said, 'Drowsy syrup!'
She said, 'Shakespeare somewhere.
Might be *Othello*.' Yev said, 'Love meeting you two.
Don't forget, crush works of Python.
Find good work. Ask Rocka Vages.'
The pair in black repeated things
like 'crush like custard powder' and 'ask Rocka,'
and Yevich was about to shake their hands
but they put arms out
and hugged him, then called as he hobbled off,
'You're awesome, man! Gud luck wi yee scaretit.'

Yevich called back, 'Thanks man!' and set off
to Ephanerothee Hospital for Men and Women of Straw

full of joy and, as he glared at
the trash of commerce, he was singing:
> *My life flows on in endless song*
> *above Earth's lamentation*
> *I hear a sweet and far-off hymn*
> *that hails a new creation.*
> *Above the tumult and the strife*
> *I hear the music ringing*
> *it sounds an echo in my soul*
> *how can I keep from singing?*

Shoppers stared,
children pointed and laughed
and he felt wrong,
a symbol of something bedraggled
from which they were trying
to drive themselves away
in their search for urban sophistication.
He tried not to let his knees
go too high like theatre puppets,
but it all made him turn away
into a sidestreet with just a newsagent
and a chain café.

In a plateglass window a poster advertised
a summer scarecrow festival
in Hazzlin Island, with music from
the Soft Shoe Gaberlunzies. In a choke of laughter
he put his hand across his mouth
to stop himself coughing out chewed kernels

on the window glass.
His shoulders jigged up and down
as he chuckled, thinking
he could make a model of himself
or Nadya for the festival competition.
He said aloud, 'Baba like image of ourselves,
like first man image of Rocka Vages.'
Yevich saw his own reflection in the window glass
and glared into the vacuity of his eyes.
He hadn't ever understood the vain fascination
for staring into mirrors
until the last few weeks,
and for a few heartbeats he saw
in himself the likeness of his brothers.

8. In the Spinning Waters

At the river near Saddleback Farm; Yevich and Python lineage is of identical nurture; other brothers; Python, without affection or gratitude, refashions himself in line with real designs of Government Standards Commission & the General Secretary's First & Second Amendments of the United Socialist State Bureaucratic & Democratic Workers' Party Law endorsed by European Federal & Congressional Reform & Constitution and semi-vertebrate farragoes firing psycho-warfare with their lying pliers and fat yip; Python's wrist watch ticks like a bomb.

* * *

A spirit of the past hung over
the Spinning Waters River.
Yevich and Python raced down the hill.
Yevich reached the millpool
a yard ahead. Python let his bag drop
and kept on running. He overtook
Yevich and jumped straight in the water.
Yevich followed, and the two brothers swam
and thrashed around
like fallen autumn branches
tossing on high waves.
When they noticed walkers approaching,
they held their breath underneath the water
until they guessed they'd passed,

then came back up
and shouted after them, 'Hello there!'
and ducked as quietly as little dace
back into the pool's depths.
They had to hold their breath longer
and sink themselves even deeper
if they saw the river bailiff
from a long way downstream
approaching in his canoe, Laughing Waters.

All summer long they darted like swallows
across the meadows of the farmland.
They found a can of Ronson lighter fuel
and discovered that by putting a match
to a trail of fuel they could flare a path
of fire across the river. As the blaze
flashed they fell on the grass laughing,
holding their stomachs,
then sniffed that their trousers
were covered in dog flup.

All that, though, seemed a long time ago.
Yevich had no lineage now, nobody
with whom he could share all this wonder
about the beauty star
Nadya Nadezhda Bukharinovna Romanov of that Nik,
and about their scaretit.
Yevich's first two brothers died three years ago
of *zulon carcinoma*, a form of wood rot –

before Nadya discovered the apricot kernels.
The first of the two brothers
were the austere Alexander,
Yevich's loyal twin with shaggy hair;
then bandy-legged Java, unhip to truth
but a genuine eccentric and Chaplinesque comedian.
Yevich's favourite brother
had been Ludvig Hezekiah
of the long and flowing hair,
one of seven thousand who also had not bowed
the knee to the RedAction Movement –
and it was rugged Ludvig Hezekiah
who was prepared to face even prosecution
in protest against the new crowscarers,
which were noisy mechanisms, a pollution,
and waste of financial resources
that railed against aesthetic tastes.
Java died in his hut last year
after cardiac arrest in the greenhouse
when the Sun had just begun to strike.
The shepherdess, Roxanna Abrodski,
didn't know whether to call the hospital,
the farmer, or a vet, as Ludvig Hezekiah
lay semi-conscious in her arms,
but in minutes he was the late Ludvig Hezekiah Romanov.
Yevich's fourth brother was Levi, tagged 'Python',
a habitual pick pocket, robber,
vandal, and the family *mouton noir*.

above the Abrodski front door

> the anger of mankind
> engendereth not
> the righteousness of God

On the grounds of their ancestors,
the farmer shepherds, Dean JW Burgon Abrodski
and his wife Roxanna Abrodski the shepherdess,
created these five brothers using tree branches,
pole handles from fire-beating brushes,
barnyard sweepers, wheelbarrow wheels for faces,
baler twine, and they stuffed grain sacks
with bulges of straw and bubble-wrap for their chests
and made them spinal cords
with discs like stalks of wheat
and they twisted hair out of old birds' nests
that had the semblance of hemisphered brains.
Roxanna Abrodski dressed them
in fading wardrobe clothes and cast-offs,
sheepskin coats, rugs and grey wolfskins.
When they were raised up from the ground,
the farmer shepherd exhaled a sigh of inspiration
that they were at last living and created
and he and Roxanna set them up
where the two rivers meet,
the Spinning Waters and the Hippie Moon River,

and these five brothers lived among us.
Each brother wore a dynastic badge
of a wolf bowing to twelve stars.
The scarecrows did Roxanna Abrodski
and Dean JW Burgon Abrodski create;
and their other deeds, are they not recorded
in the annals of
the Later Advancements of Western Intelligence?

In all his burning heart for Ludvig Hezekiah,
it was Python who was playing on Yevich's mind today.
Yevich, Alexander, Java and Ludvig Hezekiah
worked through ice and snow, gales
and baking heat in all the promised seasons
and they didn't flinch. As for Python,
his grizzled hair fell across his face
and it did him no good. His throat
was an open tomb, and he burned with hatred
for everything that's dignified and noble
and he was a red-hot activist against it,
as if it were a ritual to please some imaginary evil deity.
If anything was lofty, a mark
of high sophistication, it was a target
for Python to hurl his dirt on,
to pervert, make common and ignoble,
kitsch and populist, vulgarized and lewd,
to drag it downwards into the dust of death.
No talk, no explanation, no show
of decency towards him was able to unstring

his rage and envy. It was in the venom
of his ichor. And his ichor was up.
It was against the good foundations
and nothing would do but a lower, riff-raff mob
to hold the seat of government.
Like the destroyer of Yevich's and Nadya's country,
he craved violence: revolvers, rifles, knives,
petrol bombs, acid, anything to cause chaos.
Whatever is of beauty and comfort
to the nobler mind than his mind
must be destroyed without remembrance:
beautiful flower beds, trees and lawns and gardens,
ornate ironwork, the ballet and music
and artistry and sculptures and beautiful windows,
all things loved for centuries,
filled him with seething rage.
What fun it would be to ruin it all
with stones and fire and clubs.
He was up to devious stratagems
and into every scam and dishonest dealing.
For certain, Kleptos was his patron saint
and Kupidos his lord and rajah.
When he turned against his brothers
he mocked them as la-di-da,
called them stuck-up twats
and took off the intonations
of their superior speech.
The four brothers compared to Python
were like conflicting seeds,

as conflicting as were the Zamzummin
of the ancient Rephaim with the sons of Adam,
or like the good seed with the darnel
sowed by an enemy. Somewhere in this Python,
too, there had been false sowing;
he was a disjunct to the brotherhood.
He seemed possessed, at least, hard-bitten,
by a spirit of the Snake god,
like that fortune-telling girl in Philippi.
He constructed in his loft a floorboard
that he covered in astrocharts,
secret symbols, star signs, and the words
'Star of Remphan' painted in dripping writing,
and nobody dared to go in.

Yevich was chewing on the last
of his post-lunch apricot kernels
when he came back to his senses
and he buzzed back to the hospital,
knees pulling high in his perambulation method.

9. This could be the last time – or, One word of truth outweighs the whole world

In the maternity ward; Nadya's critical state; 'What is it but to make thy sepulchre / And creep into it far before thy time?' (*Henry the Sixth*).

* * *

All afternoon Nadya cried in agony and anguish.
Between hard breaths she was closed off to the world,
her stomach construction without sign or motion.
When she spoke it was only to say, 'So weak ...
too weak ... weak now ... now ... oh ... oh ...'
Death was certain, but she hoped
that they could save their scaretit
and she wanted to utter her last goodbye,
say to her husband to take good care of him
and of himself, say to the child about her,
about them, the scarecrow man
and the scarecrow woman who found love.

Yevich said, 'You'll be right, Nadie.'
She said, 'Ixnay, ixnay,' rolling her head.
He made a smile into the depth of her eyes,
then turned to Upper Valdaskaya,
narrowed his large round eyes and made
the minutest notion of nodding his head.

When Yevich got back to the ward after his lunch,
he found himself barred from the natal room
and made to hang around the corridor:
the father's presence might be nerve-jamming
the embarrassed mother in the birthing operation;
it's better without the husband,
especially first births.
Perhaps he wasn't going to miss anything anyway.

Upper Valdaskaya found him
by a window in the corridor
and explained the complications
and he'd better come back in.

When he saw the limpness of Nadya's body
and her frame lightly rocking
like a small boat moored along a riverbank,
his eyes filled;
he looked as if he'd seen a devil.
Underneath his breath he muttered:
    – yuh enemies of new
    yah yah gonna f-f-f-fade out.
He looked at the floor
and wished he could flob on Python's feet.
In a thin, quivering voice he whispered
to Upper Valdaskaya, 'Nadie ... Nadie die?'

A geeky-looking nurse called Geeky Nurse,
who had her hair tied back

and wore old-fashioned bull's eye glasses,
velcroed a bag around Nadya's arm
and measured her blood pressure and pulse
and said, 'Hm ... BP is not at the appropriate level ...'
and something else Yevich was unable to catch.
'That *is* low ... too low,' she said quietly,
as if only to herself.
There seems ... seems to be no ...'
Yevich said, 'But we're *scarecrows* ....'
The nurse said, 'Don't scarecrows ... ?
... So ... How is she ... ? ... How *do* you ...?'
Yevich went blank. He could have been
in a field of birds and seen nothing.

Geeky's large earrings swung heavy on her ears,
making Yevich think of primrose faces.
He thought she looked a fine piece of womanhood.

Upper Valdaskaya looked at Yevich
and said, 'Ixnay, Mr Romanov!'
She took a card out of a pocket
and she read quietly to him: 'A woman,
when she gives birth, has grief because her hour
has come, but as soon as she gives birth to the child
she remembers no more the tribulation
on account of the joy that a person
has been born into the world.'
It reminded Yevich of something,
something he'd heard or read somewhere,

maybe Booka Vax, or Gospa John.

It was gestured again he should go outside
and since he couldn't stand it all anyway
he went out to the corridor
and walked up and down, socking his palms,
then he slumped on a red plastic seat
and looked at his boots
and beat his shaggy side of sacks and rags
and prayed. A dark violin was crying in his mind.

10. To virtue add knowledge

Entomology in the maternity ward; 'Accurate language is part of the world's health, and to call something by its right name is part of true knowledge' (Thom Gunn, *Ezra Pound: Poems Selected*). Kingdoms of tall grass and fish and boondocks.

* * *

At the window of the corridor
that runs alongside the nursing station
Yevich gazed out
with the numbness of his scarecrow countenance.
The late February afternoon sunset
burned on the far hills
as if the Greeks' whole fleet of longships
had been set on licking fire by the Trojans.

The evergreen conifer western hemlock
next to the incinerator behind the emergency ward
stood proud and high, its foliage
hanging on its branches like military drapes
on ramparts of a fort. Rays of late sun
sparkled silver through the branches.

Blown against a corner of the outside window sill,
a stinghorn carcass was lying on its back.
This was of particular entomological interest to Yevich:

for ideas for patterns in his fly box
and for general insect identification,
along with serious meteorology, astronomy,
agricultural theory,
horticulture with its Latin tags and epithets,
ornithology and, to a limited extent,
ornithoscopy and natural history;
all these are attractive qualifications
for any scarecrow minding his future
with a dedicated academic approach.
Precise specification was a preoccupation
he and the late Ludvig Hezekiah had shared
just for the love of it.
He prodded the carcass around to examine it,
then drew a circle of dust around it
as for murder victims and said aloud,
'Done in by mafia boss.'

In the young Yevich
the farmer shepherds Dean and Roxanna Abrodski
had seen some spark above most workers,
and from time to time they made Yevich conscious
of the descriptive *Georgics* of the poet Virgil:
'What makes the corncrops glad,
under which star to turn the soil,'
and so he knew what it is to 'strip to plough,
and strip to sow,' and they taught him
how great Virgil says that everything
by Nature's law devolves into a backward state

so has to be stripped back or cultivated,
although he could hardly bear the noise
of the field machines' rattling on golden autumn evenings
when trout were on the rise.

More than Virgil, though, Yevich
liked Gilbert White
whose *Natural History of Selborne* edition
proclaims that Selborne is
the private parish inside us all.
The things of White's *Selborne* held for Yevich
greater fascination than even Virgil.
Yevich would unfold his edition of reader notes
(translated back into English from a rare Russian version
by Lev Matushkin), and browsed over these:

~ of his vast knowledge on many subjects, particularly birds, and his method of obtaining knowledge:
* 'After so much labour is bestowed in erecting a mansion, as nature seldom works in vain, martins will breed on for several years together in the same nest, where it happens to be well sheltered and secure from the injuries of weather. The shell or crust of the nest is a sort of rustic work full of knobs and protuberances on the outside: nor is the inside of those that I have examined smoothed with any exactness at all; but is rendered soft and warm, and fit for incubation, by a lining of small straws, grasses, and feathers; and sometimes by a bed of moss interwoven with wool. In this nest they tread, or engender, frequently during the time of building; and the hen lays from three to five white eggs;
* of the 'sociality' of animals and birds: 'There is a

wonderful spirit of sociality in brute creation, independent of sexual attachment: the congregating of gregarious birds in the winter is a remarkable instance';

~ his theological and philosophical reasonings about 'brute creation' and mankind:
* 'I lay it down as a maxim in ornithology, that as long as there is any incubation going on there is music'; 'Two great motives which regulate the proceedings of the brute creation are love and hunger; the former incites animals to perpetuate their kind, the latter induces them to preserve individuals; whether either of these should seem to be the ruling passion in the matter of congregating is to be considered. As to love, that is out of the question at the time of the year when that soft passion is not indulged; besides, during the amorous season, such a jealousy prevails between the male birds that they can hardly bear to be together in the same hedge. Most of the singing and elation of spirits of that time seem to me to be the effect of rivalry and emulation: and it is to this spirit of jealousy that I chiefly attribute the equal dispersion of birds in the spring over the face of the country'

He had come across that idea nowhere else.
'Love and hunger,' Yevich said aloud,
turning the book over on his lap.
'Nadya, Nadya all my love and hunger!
'Sounds like poem.
Love and hunger, food of music.
Thought music was for play ... Haha!
Thought music was foreplay.
Thought music was ...'

He had to stuff an arm in his mouth
to imprison any boom of laughter.
'Why I'm here! But pains of labour,
not place for laugh.'
He got up to the window
and flicked the stinghorn carcass
along the window ledge
and it spun to a standstill.
'Nah more love and music for you,
Señor Stinghorn ... Or Señora Stinghorn.
How your babies born, then?'
He turned the book over again:

* 'sexual diversity [of birds] does not take place in earlier life; for a beautiful youth shall be so like a beautiful girl that the difference shall not be discernible'

He always laughed at that.
Yevich cared not for the discerning
of the usefulness of gender of a bird:
they all have to get off.
He laughed as well that a boy
could look as beautiful as a girl.
'Nadya pretty scarecrow girl.
Nothing like a boy. Imagine it! Ugh!'

~ use of words: 'nidification', nesting, from French *nid*; 'nidicolous', longer than average in the nest; 'altricial', hatching immature; 'precocial', hatching quite mature;
* bird language too, and bird 'vocabulary'

~ of people: the mad bee boy village idiot: 'In the winter he dosed away his time, within his father's house, by the fireside, in a kind of torpid state, seldom departing from the chimney-corner; but in the summer he was all alert, and in quest of his game in the fields, and on sunny banks ... Honey-bees, humble-bees, and wasps were his prey wherever he found them: he had no apprehension from their stings, but would seize them *nudis manibus* and at once disarm them of their weapons, and suck their bodies for the sake of their honey-bags ... As he ran about he used to make a kind of humming noise with his lips, resembling the buzzing of bees ... When a tall youth he was removed from hence to a distant village where he died, as I understand, before he arrived at manhood.'

'Poor mad bee boy dead. Look at this.'
A surgeon in a green overall
and a green facemask was hurrying past
as if for an emergency.
Stuttering his paces, he said, 'What ...
what boy, Mister Gallyblagger?'
Yevich raised his book and pointed to the page,
saying, 'Boy died. Selborne bee boy.'
The surgeon made his apology and hurried on.
Yevich shouted after him, 'Not going to
Nadya Nadezhda Bukharinovna Romanov
of that Nik, are you? My Nadie all right?'
The man disappeared
through flapping rubber doors.

Yevich pulled his hat over his conkers
and prayed: 'Rocka Vages,

give Nadie Stakhanovite energy.'

And if Yevich were going to have three to feed, though there was no certainty of that right now, any knowledge might be a most delicious thing and not the most unsweetest thing.

11. Scales of Python

While Yevich waits in the corridor, Nadya still deep in care in the labour room with Upper Valdaskaya; Yevich's mind and sewing machine heart stitched with memories of the day when in a cosmic heartbeat of deep time vengeance cracked its arthritic knuckles and rammed its sword between Earth and Heaven and Python got barbecued and two Colombian imports sloped off like twin wolves snarling at the edge of a moor and the wind whipcracked from the East and rode side-saddle across the valley. That night a star the size of a gasometer sank over the Saddlebacks and a mist rose from the fields like the zorst pipes of a yammahamma and the dark violin played its smoky music in the valley. Fighting in the barn at Saddleback Farm; the grass is growing as we speak.

   * * *

Isayevich Ishi Romanov turned
from the window
and said aloud, as if his wife were present,
'Yev going to have to rise to it, Nadie.
Yev going to have to get off his fife an' drum, Nadie,'
repeating things he'd told her
on the tractor in the morning.

He slipped Gilbert White back
in his jacket and picked up

a hospital waiting-room magazine
which was stamped with the hospital name
in a stylish font,
as if it were a thing the hospital did not wish to lose
or be taken. It wasn't White or Virgil
but he thumbed through it,
relieved to be distracted from anxiety
for Nadya. It hovered between prolefeed
and health guidance. Photographs
and a report of the wedding
of a princess, as fresh as is the rose of May.
An article, The Zinc Spark:
'An explosion of tiny sparks erupts
from the egg at the exact moment
of conception.' Funny people.
With what slow seasons
the waiting-room clock was moving
its wheel of fortune.

The sprawl and utter lifelessness of that stinghorn
screenplayed in Yevich's head
the day when he found Python …

Python, bother to Yevich but not
a brother, the scheming reprobate,
one of the בנים בליעל — *beni belial* —
sons of uselessness:
he failed to conduct himself

like a true son of the field
and walked around in stab-proof oxhide vests.

The great lion of justice
and the serpent of evil
would bite each other's tails
and the balances had poised precariously
for long enough and spared Python,
but one deed of his treachery
might bring hard vengeance
so that the right-hand pan
of the scales would come clanging
and the balances drop out of his favour.

According to a witness
who had been walking in a neighbouring field,
the blacksmith Biff Zhukovsky from Moonshee Cottage,
the most trusted man in the district,
it happened this way ...
On a midweek morning the previous autumn,
dawn rose over the Saddlebacks in her pink jeans
and blood-red cotton headbands,
trailing long purple scarves across the hills,
and the early Sun had a grandstand seat.
Two rival ruffians from the miasma
of the underground world
that Python swirled about in, two men
mad for fighting, concealed themselves
early in the half light like ghosts

inside a bush, as Hixmanus
and Callipygous concealed themselves
in the day when great Vim perished
as he strolled beside the lake
behind his war bivouac, or as Odysseus
and Diomedes hid among slain bodies
before they slaughtered Dolon, Hector's boldest messenger.
This pair of big men crept behind Python,
all along a hedgerow they were creeping,
until they reckoned he was out of public sight,
then they sprang out and ran at him.
One held him round the neck with a wrestler's grip
and the other unsheathed a silver butcher's knife
he'd stolen from a discount drug store set
and let Python have it,
blammed it like a lightning bolt
and it flashed into a point
between the shoulder joints of Python,
splitting the grain sack and chest stuffing
with a crunch that made him scream
and his arms flung up
and rays of agony lacerated his senses
so that his wooden legs buckled at the knee joints
and he staggered like a wounded animal
dragging a crazy spear in its belly,
then he crumpled against a hedge
and the pirate-bearded hitman
with the razor-sharp knife
jabbed the side of his guts

and twisted it in
and down foul Python fell
with a thump,
crashing head-first into the ditch of dying gloom,
sunk into consciousness shut-down,
pumping his last heartbeats in deep time,
and he groaned, blind to daylight,
until death discovered the doorway in his brain
and numb darkness wrapped him in a shroud
and nobody was sorry. The assassin,
rumoured to be from Colombia,
stamped his boot on Python's back
and disgorged his bolt-long knife,
wet with wine-dark oil,
and they left him for red kites
and crows to peck at.

That was the evidence of Biff Zhukovsky.
The stenographer, who had little interest
in the case, recorded him
as Ziff Bhukovsky from Moonshy Cottage.

Around noontime, Yevich found dead Python,
before the birds could tear his eyes out,
before maggots and marauding hordes of flies
could wriggle through his clothing
and corrode his corpse. Yevich lifted him
in a horse cart, and tied
a pale wagon cover over the body

and drove him home on the cart
with its wheels clattering on the track
and as he rode along with solemnity
the horse's mane ruffled in the wind.
Dean and Roxanna Abrodski burned
Python's carcass in a purifying fire.

The witness kept all this to herself
for several days in case she came under suspicion,
until she realized that her telephone signal
could get tracked at the location,
then she did come under suspicion
when it was said she'd been identified
more than once outside Python's cottage
getting out of a window-tinted car
in the company of a drugs lord.

Just as Yevich was wanting to shake his head
free of these images, he was made to jump
at violent sounds of agony
like a screech owl
coming from one of the women
in the labour wards, maybe Ginger Pitchfork,
not Nadya's room, Yevich realized,
but his heart was thumping.
He was wanting to lose himself
in thoughts of Nadya,
the night he knew he'd fallen for her
at the village hall when she was playing

Alguinaldo Cayeyano in A minor in Db minor
on her ten-stringed Cuatro de Puertorriqueño
and then singing *La Musica E Por La Noche*.
Yevich spoke to her at the drinks bar:
'You play, it beautiful.
You play eight semitones
lower than standard A minor.'
She said, 'Well, Mister Romanov,
I call it five semitones higher.'
Yevich laughed a little more than it was funny.
'You on *fire*! Fire of Russian music!' Yevich glared
in her eyes. 'You *indagatrix*
on Cuatro de Puertorriqueño.
Indagatrix es.' She raised her beer mug
to his mug and they clinked glasses
and she said, '*Haruspex es*.'
He said, '*Haruspex! Ego? Cur, cur* you say ...?
She said, 'Because you said *sum indagatrix*.'
They clinked their beer mugs again.
He said, 'Nadya Nadezhda Bukharinovna Romanov
of that Nik, you box office!'
She said, 'It's Spanish music. The loving tongue.'
He said, 'Cuatro de Puertorriqueño sounds like balalika.'
'No, no,' she said, 'not like a balalika really,
Mister Romanov, not really.'

The gentleness of her correction did him in
and he walked home telling the night sky.
He repeated over and over 'No, no, not like a balalika

really, Mister Romanov, not really.'
'Too good, too good she is!
Phoebus' sister! Might she be
"of my lyf and deeth the queene"?
Flower of all queens! Her old blue hat.
Her yellow trousers, and those patches.'
                                     In his kitchen
he prepared everything he needed
for being in the fields before sunrise
and that unbearable mocking chorus of the dawn,
from the daughters of music
and lords of the wing,
which would not be like the sweet music
of that female gallyblagger's D flat
Alguinaldo Cayeyano balalaika heaven,
then he collapsed on his bed like a puppet.
He was trying to read something about
In Praise of Character in the Bleak Inhuman Loneliness
For twenty minutes he picked up the book
and put it down again. At midnight
he gave up and went to the kitchen.
All he could manage was to stare
into the middle distance,
and he stood like that
until it was time to go and terrify the birds.

Now, on a day he ought to be rejoicing,
his head was burning
with these recollections of the late Python

and his pregnant wife was dying.
A man in a boiler suit
pushing a trolley and holding a delivery note
walked past singing,
Johnny's in the basement mixing up the medicine,
I'm on the pavement thinking about the ...
Yevich didn't catch the last word.
He said to the man, 'What strange song! *What* medicine?'
The man looked back at Yevich,
smiled, and walked on.
Yevich wished he knew the song,
the rest of the words.
What medicine? Thinking about *what*?

Hard as it was for Yevich to lose a brother,
whatever his character as a בני בליעל
– *beni belial* – a son of uselessness,
Python's death was double-edged.
A few years ago, Yevich, coming off duty,
with a sprig of montbretia in his straw hat,
met Python at the organic farm signboard
and they walked the track together
talking casually. Low fires burned
around the cow sheds to scare off
a recent plague of sharp-fanged snakes
that might shrink from the bright daylight
and slither in and stab the herd's legs
with their venom. Python followed

Yevich in a barn, where rows of bats
hung upside-down like greasy tractor rags
and with their evil grin. Python made out
as if he were going to practice
on a dartboard and, as Yevich
carried a large trough of horse fodder
across the floor, Python knocked his legs off balance,
shuffled him across the floor
and pinned him to a wall,
twisted his shirt underneath his throat
and gripped his neck, pressing
his fingers under Yevich's ears,
making Yevich splutter and causing choking sounds
as he was losing consciousness.
Python made some threat,
beginning 'Listen, Captain Hook …',
which Yevich assumed some smart-arse joke
alluding to his fishing, but he didn't understand
whatever it was Python was blurting about:
something about not saying anything
to Dean Abrodski
concerning the number of cars and tractors
parked outside Python's cottage yesterday,
but Yevich hadn't seen any cars all day,
although two weeks ago he'd seen cars
and people mingling, and some monstrous man
like a tattooed Queequeg in dark glasses
who seemed to be giving out orders.
As soon as Python released his grip

on Yevich's throat so that he could speak
an answer to Python's threat, Yevich,
his heart shaking like a field of beaten corn,
flew a hand up and clamped it over Python's face
and drew him to the floor. He clambered a knee
on Python who started whimpering
and said he was only playing and it was all a joke.
Yevich told him, 'You act out life
like worst vulgar subnograph
led by subnograph of subnographs.'
Python said back, 'Times are chagrin
for your stuck-up lot of twats.'
Yevich stuttered, 'Says in Virgil,
the underworld hopes not for you as king.'
After a few philosophical words of advice
on how to conduct oneself in life,
which aphorisms and homilies he prefaced
with epithets and phrases,
Yevich released his brother,
let him to his feet,
and pushed him hard out of the barn,
shouting, 'Uncircumcised Philistine!'
Barnyard dust clung on Python's back
and he rubbed the side of his face
and went muttering like a sloping wolf
with a rattling tin can tied to its tail.

After that, Python would look across
with a dirty sullen face at Yevich

and make a cutting motion
across his throat. Yevich warned Nadya
never to allow Python entrance
through their door. If she passed him
in the lane, she allowed him scarcely a smile
and tried not to let him notice nervousness.

A week before Python's death, the late afternoon
was crackling with lightning
and thunder rolled along the Saddleback Hills
and shook the land
and the neighbouring house lights
flickered on and off. Yevich was in the barn
preparing stall covers for an event,
an organic fortnight with a soil association connection –
he wasn't sure of the details –
when he noticed Python leering at a wood axe
as he hovered by the doorway.
Yevich stuck a boot in Python's step
and gave his shoulder a violent shove
and Python splattered in the rain-drenched dust outside.
As when Odysseus came to the camp edge
of the weary Thracians and their king
and loosed the tethers of their snowy horses
from their chariot rail, and used his bow
to whack their white behinds and drive them off,
so Yevich hauled Python from the ground
and smacked his backside with a spade
to make him scurry out of sight and reach.

Yevich held the axe by his side
and watched Python's slow skulk.

12. Nadie done baba, Nadie?

Nadya in the labour room flipped out; Yevich in the corridor learns how women suffer; things get bodging; the next generation brought to light in the Ephanerothee Hospital for Men and Women of Straw; Brautigan: 'Gee, you're so beautiful that it's going to rain'; Blake: 'the jewel health adorns her neck'.

    * * *

It wasn't until five it seemed
a birth might appear.
Her hands gripped the sides of the bed.
Upper Valdaskaya was urging,
'Push, push Nadya, push ...'
Nadya could only pant thinly:
'Can't ... haven't ... not ... strength left,'
then her body relaxed into stillness.

As Upper Valdaskaya opened the door
of the labour room to find Yevich,
a deathly yell rushed out of Nadya's throat.
Yevich leapt to his feet.
The yell made his heart-box stop
and stung his ears, and watered his eyes.

Upper Valdaskaya said, 'It's all right, Mister Romanov,

your scaretit should be coming soon.'
Yevich gazed at the floor.
He said, '*Should?*', eyes still on the floor.
A scream came from another room.
Upper Valdaskaya said: 'Birthing's painful, Mr Romanov.
He jackknifed himself up
and put his hands in the small
of his back, arching against the stiffness.

Geeky Nurse took Nadya's arm
and was about to check for a pulse,
but as she reached for her wrist
the nurses witnessed the top of
a small felt-textured purple globe appearing
in the open oyster of her eternal circle of birth,
her small rubber tyre from a child's tricycle.
She exhaled a mighty groan,
and a small form shot through
as if squeezed from a tube of toothpaste,
then flopped in Valdaskaya's hands.

Valdaskaya and Geeky nudged each other away
in a playful rivalry to cut the cord.
Valdaskaya, being the senior, gave way
and handed a tough pair of scissors to Geeky.

When Nadya had been washed and comforted
Valdaskaya told Geeky to get Yevich in.
He walked straight to Nadya,

held her hand and kissed her head
and said, 'Done it, Nadie Bukharinovna.
Done baba come!'

He said thank you to Valdaskaya
and Geeky Nurse, holding them in turn
in a tight grip, and took a seat
by Nadya's bedside and fixed his eyes
on his wriggling son, while Valdaskaya
and Geeky Nurse cleaned the scaretit
and wrote notes on clipboards
and Yevich looked at the curious squiggles
and wished he could write
long medical words.
        Nadya undid her duffle coat buttons
and unthreaded a criss-cross strip of leather
and uncovered two porridge sacks
hanging like a horse's nose bag.
She drew her scaretit to feed
as is its divinely born instinct.
The scaretit put his lips over the warm oats
and sucked in. When he turned his face
once towards his father, he saw an oily trickle
of creamy liquid smeared on the scaretit's cheek
putting Yevich in mind
of the come-uppance fluid
that had begun Nadya's and Yevich's new generation,
and of how Jimmy – for the haze of it all
he couldn't remember why now –

took him outside during their wedding reception
and pointed to the Moon
and told him women sometimes like it slow.
You don't just gratify yourself.
Even now Yevich wasn't sure.
He looked as if he were the man Adam
on the first morning of creation,
just born out of dust himself,
and seeing unspoiled Eden for the first time
as his newborn eyes were opening.

He was buffaloed by all the technical apparatus,
the forms and gadgets, Nadya's oxygen mask.
Geeky Nurse put a cloth over a silver tray
that should have been taken away before;
in it were the umbilical cord
that was like baler twine
and some grisly stuff which reminded her of trout guts.
Geeky took it away,
relieved that Yevich hadn't seen it.

Yevich's and Nadya's firstborn
was a rosy scaretit, bright as a shining star.
Upper Valdaskaya and Geeky Nurse
fixed the infant scarecrow up
from the bag of clothes Nadya had prepared:
a badger-striped blazer with red wood buttons
the size of an ezra piece,
chunky brown corduroy trousers one size too big,

and his straw feet they tucked in bonny white socks,
and over the socks they tied a pair
of mini imitations of his dad's work boots,
then put a jaunty trilby on his head.

Nadya splashed water on her face
from a handbowl.
                    For forty minutes
Yevich watched everybody's proceedings
and thought profound things in scarecrow thoughts.
Valdaskaya handed the scaretit to Yevich.
The scarecrow man could hardly speak.
He'd never seen a scaretit before.
He said a wooden 'Hello', then pressed on
the little thing's legs and arms,
kissed his head and put him on his lap.
He stroked the side of his face
and said, 'Done baba come,'
and then 'Goo-Gaga,'
and went on saying, 'Goo-Gaga,' over and over.
He was like a robot awakened out of his condition.
He hummed the tune then sang in a soft voice,
'Rock-a-bye scaretit in the tree tops'.
He touched the scaretit's tiny straw feet,
felt the soft fontanelle Nadya told him about,
and sat and held his son with the pride
of the first parents on Earth.
A few fine little twigs were springing
out of the scaretit's head like a crown of thorns.

Yevich thought about the rooks
and what their scaretit might become,
and he pronounced a blessing:
'*Asher-eh ha ish asher lo halak ba assat reshayim,*'
which from the tongue of the Davidic psalm is
'Oh the happinesses of the man who has not walked
in the counsel of the wicked.'
And he said, 'No Python wickedness misery
for Goo-Gaga, please, Rocka Vages.'
Valdaskaya looked with a deep question mark,
and Yevich said, 'Jimmy taught me,'
then he looked into his scaretit's blue eyes
and said, 'Say *shoo*. Say *shoo, shoo birdies.*'
Goo-Gaga cried, '*Waa, waa, waaaa,*'
and his father said, 'Not quite there yet,
is it, Geeky Nurse? Hasn't got it yet.
Got to scare 'em off.
It's *whaa-ha-ha*, not *waa, waa, waaaa.*'
Nobody said anything.

Yevich put the scaretit back
on the pink kiss apples
of Nadya's porridge sacks.

Yevich stroked Nadya's head
and cast his look between her eyes
and Goo Gaga.
'Good lunch, Yev?' she asked him
as he moved his hand to hold her arm.

'Good, good, Nadie. Organic salad, custard tart.'
She said, '*Custard*! Got milk, Yev.
Milk for baba goo-gaga cows, not us.
We don't suckle under udders of another species.
All organic on Saddleback Farm.
Two fingers up at poison pharma drugs
and World Sick Dot Org.'
Yevich jerked his head round
to see if Upper Valdaskaya was listening.
'Yeah, forgot, Nadie. Bit excited.'

13. Fries my wig, Roxanna

The hinges swing back on the gates of Eden and,
metaphor in hand, Yevich proclaims the firstborn to
the Universe; if ya frown too much wear a bandana.

* * *

While Nadya was having stitches
where her body was gashed
like the Saddleback Hills sunset,
Yevich went out to the corridor
to ring the shepherdess.
Said the scarecrow, 'Hosanna? You?'
Said the shepherdess, '*Rox*, *Rox*-anna Abrodski.'
And Yevich said, 'Hip-hosanna, Roxanna!
It Yevich Romanov. Hosanna Roxanna!
Nadie done baba. Done baba come. Done baba come.
Nadie done baba ... the goo-gaga.
Done done done, baba baba come.
Yev ding-dong daddy. Ring them bells!
Fries my wig! Dancing bananas, mama!
Blood and oxygen, mama! Tell Dean Burgon.'
'Well how absolutely marvellous,
darling!' said the shepherdess.
'What have you called him?'
And the scarecrow said, 'Goo-Gaga, I think.'
And the shepherdess said, 'What a *lovely* name!
Another Romanov. Goo-Gaga Romanov of that Nik.

Aquila non edit muscas. The eagle does not eat flies.
The birth of language. Here comes Goo-Gaga.
Here comes Goo-Gaga Abrodski Romanov.
A hard life improves the vision. Cosmic, cosmic!
Does he have Latin?' And Yevich said, '*Quid erat hoc?*
You funny, you like groovy granny!'
And said the scarecrow, 'I told Goo-Gaga,
"Say *shoo, shoo birdies,*" but Goo-Gaga cried, "*Waa, waa,*"
so I told him, "Not quite there, Goo-Gaga."
Hasn't got it yet. It's *whaa-ha-ha,* not *waa-waa-wa!*'
And the shepherdess said,
'You are a very funny gallyblagger.'
And the scarecrow said, 'Izzatso? Nurses smiling –
heard them.'
Roxanna Abrodski said, 'Sorry?'

When he went back to Nadya's room
somebody had sellotaped
a no-entry notice on her door.
He socked his palms and ambled
up and down the hospital corridor
whistling Beethoven's *Ode to Joy,*
then switched tunes to the opening bars
of Bach's *Jesu, Joy of Man's Desiring,*
so softly it was scarcely heard,
then back to *Ode to Joy,*
tapping the rhythms on his hip.

He thought about the time last year

the farmer shot 153 rooks
in one afternoon after the farmer found them
in a field, lined up like Trojan squadrons
being shouted up by Hector for a battle.
While Yevich was off doing peripatetic work
the rooks destroyed half a field's beet in two days.
If there were no scarecrows to guard
the fields constantly, then – no crops;
and if no crops – no people;
and if no people – nobody to employ scarecrows.
In that case, the rook and crow
are the great enemy of the country
and the scarecrow is its saviour,
hanging, dead to the world, arms wide
as if in supplication for the shire.
The world can throw its arms out
to save itself when it trips,
but from the greater fall it cannot save itself.

Yevich was feeling his belly-sack
rumbling with the thunder of hunger,
as he sat in the waiting-room area
of the maternity ward
of the Ephanerothee Hospital for Men and Women
of Straw
and, as the rubber doors flapped shut
and open with the current of people
along the corridor which generations passed
like the river of God,

Yevich Isayevich Romanov had visions
of Nadya Nadezhda Bukharinovna Romanov.

He clunked himself off the waiting-room seat
and pressed coins in a thin metallic slot
and leaned the odd contraption
of his own frame against the drinks machine.
The smack of a plastic cup
dropping on a plate startled him.
Dark coffee streamed into the cup.
He lifted out the cup, careful
not to knock it on the machine
and spill the dark liquid, and he put his nose
to its edge to sniff the coffee mixture
but swished his head away in revulsion.
He replaced the cup of foul stuff
back on the dispensing plate,
and in doing that caught a sharp reflection
of himself in the fascia of the drinks machine,
himself in the image of himself,
reproduced, like his son reproduced in his image.
He said, 'Hello, me,' and smiled,
and, 'Hello, me again. Me again again,'
then frowned when the image clouded over
with his breath. He rubbed it
with a jacket sleeve. The smell of his exhalation
rebounded in his face. 'Ah, ah,' he said,
'smell like the Saddleback Hills. Like Nadie's breath.
Like earth and worms. Like cow hoof-dented soil

of the fields.' When he saw the scruffiness
of his mop-head hair his Charlie Chaplin beam
dropped into another frown.
He made faces at himself in the fascia,
poking his tongue and blowing his cheeks out
like the west wind,
turning his body and tilting his head
in mockery of a vain model in a photo-shoot.
An old scarecrow favourite song from days of old
came to his mind
and an overwhelming blast of joy elevated him
and he let his knee and elbow joints rise,
with the weight falling mostly on his good leg
and as his joints fell and rose
in a clumsy and clattering dance
he sang in a strong Russian accent:

> *No strings da-da da da da-da*
> *da da-da da-da, da da-da da-da*
> *I'm not made of wood*
> *I don't have a wooden heart*

He saw again his reflection in the steel plate.
The selection panel said this robotic machine thing
dispensed organic fruit juices,
so Yevich slid a bolchek coin down the thing's throat
and pressed the button for a large carton
of apple juice, and he sat down
and thought about Nadya
and he thought about little Goo-Gaga,
and he thought about Python

and the words of the late Python's RedAction songs
and, as he sipped his organic juice through a thin straw,
a phrase was throbbing in his head,
'bad star rising', then more phrases,
so he got a pen and paper and a funny look
from a passing male nurse
and scratched down notes towards a poem:

> *bad star rising   spirit of Python*
> *misty phantom of new*
> *good kosmic order disappearing*
> *world is broken wheel*
> *need something strong to smash*
> *Goliath's stupid brow*
> *what of the bedraggled ones?*
> *what of the bedraggled ones who thrust*
> *vigorous shoulder to the field*
> *ripe for harvest?*
> *but Python dead*
> *bad star – but ha, brand new son*

bad star – but ha, brand new son

14. The Earth was void and without form

At Saddleback Farm; Meditations on a Trout in a meditation called Meditation on the Trout Who Faces Downstream in Tilmore Brook; safe-cracking the enigma of what to do on Earth to hoard the haggis while vegetating on the Master Plan & who's going to be the Zygo all these blonde long years & knock yer eyes out was like demystifying the night sky.

    * * *

When Yevich worked as under-assistant
at the pick-your-own organic farm,
customers who gathered produce felt obliged
to discuss farming ethics,
farm practices, prices, back ache,
and half-baked weather checks. The scarecrows
let them do most of the talking.
The customers rarely hung back for responses,
just passed along, as soon as they'd done with chattering,
to the nearest frame of blueberries.

There was, for Yevich, his cottage to maintain,
the musket he was renovating to sell to some dealer,
his trout fishing in the summer
and the Mayfly Carnival of the early warm months
when the mist of an olive hatch hovers over the water
and trout lose all their senses;

and he had the overture of cello music from the river
he could listen to from his window.
A small cactus from Mexico rested
in a clay vase on the windowsill.
He'd been considering a weekend at Christchurch
where he could take out a licence
for sea trout on the River Avon.

By the time the last customer
had his basket weighed
and was starting up his car
or walking down the track
with his heavy load of fruit
staining his garments,
Yevich was relaxing on a bench by the weighing shed
and swiping away mosquitoes.
He scanned the hills and sky
when the evening Sun burned
on the fields of wheat
and every stalk and ear flashed
like a golden jewel on a king's crown.
He picked himself a few berries,
cut a cob for supper
and wiped his Long John Silver knife
on a tuft of grass,
while the day's trailing end blazed with scythes of fire
on the furthest darkening hill
of Valhalla's kitchen's feasting ovens
and its excruciating anthracitic fires;

he watched everything around him
till the heavenly plough came to rest
in the late night sky.
In the early sunset of the cold months
the winter world looked
tearfully beautiful in snow.

In the summer evening sunsets
he thought often of the lines
of the bedraggled man
of Dove Cottage: 'The wise man, I affirm,
can find no rest / In that
which perishes.' But men and scarecrows
perish with the rest,
so what was the use or sense of that?

For all this, though, for all this might
and beauty, he registered in the complexities of his guts
and central nervous system a deep dispossession,
and there was no one
to discuss these things with
or make sense of them.
In the autumn, shooting stars blasted their way
through space at 135,000 miles an hour
above the calm, still Earth,
leaving a glowing streak in their wake,
shedding, he supposed, clouds of dust,
like the tears of St Lawrence. He had no idea
if its smoking trail of signals might be speaking

something, somewhere, somehow, some sign,
or even if it was all meant to mean anything,
if it was meant to be interpreted.
He was a traveller driving
into the western night
and he didn't know how to stop.

It was more than the hollow rib of loneliness:
it was a spiritual vacuousness
that he was only able to extrapolate,
to estimate from known values,
in terms of unfulfilled ambitions,.
and even these were immeasurable –
for the multiple practical considerations
that civilisation has constructed
fall short of the mark that men's spirits
are pressing down on them
and make demands of them to seek out
whatever infinity might hide behind
the investigation of these superior considerations.
What was true for wise humanity
could also be true for bedraggled men.

He knew the *Von Bardovian Explanation
of Kosmokratology: Definitions of Rulership & Populating
of the Earth According to Geological & Prophetic Eons* –
and it was elementary to perceive the conclusions
and fulfilling of the prophecies,
and the chieftains only want to drag

the Earth and its fullness down
into thinking just like they do.
And he knew, too, the *Lucian and Von Bardovian
Binary Theory of Hypnographics and Subnography*,
for example, how those of Berea
were more fair-minded, daily checking
the Scrolls to see if things were true,
but being one of the bedraggled, the riff-raff,
the unworthy, he didn't have a clue
where to position himself
in the contemporary jostle
since the poisoned wells
of the Bubonic RedAction Movement,
when everyone was made to lose
and bend their minds
and no longer recognize their station
or the validity of their own minds
other than the fairy-tales of the approved party line.
Yet those curiosities he'd read
in Aubrey's *Brief Lives*
only impressed on him all the more
the futility of the universal effort
to reach beyond the elemental.
If only to understand that these ephemera
are tutors. How, though, could he know any process
of selectivity, what material rejection
in attainment of what immaterial,
what abstraction, if, as is generally supposed,
that *is* any signal towards true light?

And how, inside the great canyon of the mind,
does the conscience scream between two poles,
like the war-craft twice every day
between dark and light,
so that the mind is in irons
and no sacrifice of smoking goat flesh
is ever able to lift the plague?

On many August evenings he'd seen the Sun,
like a mighty warrior,
hurl its spears of light at its dark foe
the night, and shatter it –
sometimes the night would stab the sky red;
sometimes the day would cloak it white.
The agriculturists of ancient time
would read all these as auguries
and combine it with their ornithoscopy
to make prophecies for the crops.
He knew Achilles spoke with power
and wisdom when he said 'no riches
can compare with being alive', but Yevich
could press philosophy and thought no further.
A customer told him a stone
from the southern region of Babylon
records the ages of Sumerian kings
as being between 11,000 and 72,000 years –
but were those shorter years
than our calendar years,
or is the stone a fiction?

He had no way of knowing –
but if only, throughout so many millennia,
there at least might be just one person
to systematize the arrangements
of one's lower matters ...

Two years ago came promotion
unexpectedly to chief minder
on the fields of beet.
That uphill-sloping aspect of the farm
gave him a better view of the Saddlebacks,
but, more than that, he'd served
a long apprenticeship, and now
the elevated status with its added
responsibilities seemed to be the beginning
of something filling up inside him.
From his bedroom window he passed many hours
staring over fields.

One evening on the cart track,
after a kick-around behind the old cow sheds
during a black coffee and apple break,
Yevich was sitting in the Prattle Shed
with the labourers and Heinz 'Jimmy' VonLunnhaus,
longest serving of the farm workers,
who had an iron hook. Yevich said
to him, 'Jimmy, man, I'm not myself.
I'm like Romeo, but not with pining love.'
Jimmy said to go with him

to his nephew's wedding.

While the partners signed the register,
Yevich picked a Scroll out from the pew
and read a chapter near the end.
He was about to bang his hands
and clap like thunder,
but Jimmy's iron hook pressed down
on his hands, and Yevich whispered
to him, 'Good story. Dead man ... came back!'
He walked out of the chapel
and looked across the village green
and its small community, and in an atom of time
he glimpsed a thing inexpressible,
a direction in the eternal arrow
of linear history,
in that some among the dead might rise,
and in knowing just that he felt a part,
a belonging, a substance, in a great clanking chain
that was dragging
towards a metaphysical ecstasy,
something ten million birdsongs and farms away
from everything that came to pass on Earth.
The stone of blind confusion seemed
to roll away. He said to Jimmy,
'Jimmy, *like* that Scroll, Jimmy!
Like that Rocka Vages, Jimmy!'
Jimmy put a hand on Yevich's shoulder.
For Yevich it was as if, forking out of the heavens,

knowledge and understanding fizzed
in a single bolt of lightning
of everything in history and the mind
that either enervates or makes glad
the higher spirit
and it seemed as if new voltages
were regenerating the entire mechanics
and spirit of him.
He opened wide his arms
and the billion times ten billion megawatts of light
flooded his pulsating mind.
It was as when the solar wind
collides with the Earth's magnetic field
of oxygen and nitrogen atoms
and the sky displays an aurora theatre show
of the spectacle of the throne of God,
rolling colours in a miracle
of particle physics – that was all
a fraction only of the miracle
of the Scroll's exquisite grammar.

When he set his eyes
on the beauty star Nadya Bukharinovna
for the first time, the epiphany was multiplying.
There'd been pretty girls enough,
bedraggled girls of straw,
part-time workers at the pick-your-own fruit farm,
who tremored his equanimity
and he enjoyed for six months

a hoo-ha with Angelica,
but she turned out a queen of diamonds
and desire misted up his eyes
and wisdom and he were far adrift.
Then Nadya Bukharinovna, who worked in the gardens
of Tollemache House, emanated a spirit
beyond them all. Then came the day
that he stuttered to her along the path,
from the other side of hedges,
'If you would say me nay, please reconsider.'
Like Hannah, mother of the prophet Samuel,
her lips moved, but no voice was heard.

15. Wedding of the scarecrows

Yevich and Nadya dungfork solitude and get rewired and 'never weather-beaten sail more willing bent to shore' (Campion); they swarfega off the existential headache and get jizzed and joyous and jangle each other's head with happy-sounding sweetness.

   * * *

Within seven months of his meeting
Nadya Nadezhda Bukharinovna,
her husband Isayevich Romanov and she
were walking out of the chapel
hanging on each other's straw fingers,
she rose-cheeked, her head adorned
in delicate flora, the young, noble frame
of her figure white-gowned,
the glory of Russia.
On a day when the montbretia was blazing,
the August sunshine turned itself on them
and the summer breeze passed above their heads
and strummed its harp music
of the sea and Moon
as the church rang beyond the stars
a glad windblown folksong on its bells.

The bride's and bridegroom's colleagues
made an arch of honour

with hoes and rakes and draves and spakes.
Nadya turned from one implement carrier to another
clasping her hand across her mouth
as she laughed, taken aback in joy.

It would have required the philosophers of Greece
to describe Yevich's state of mind.
If you saw his eyes, you saw the whole story.
He was, perhaps, of one mind astonished
that it should be he standing one soul with Nadya,
he who felt so long a common sparrow
among the eminent falcons and eagles of society,
he who, now, with Nadya Nadezhda Bukharinovna
was on the grass bank of the chapel,
gazed up at by the village –
and he was, perhaps, of another mind
that he ought to be displaying a dignity
that was fitting. His three-piece suit itched.
It was too heavy for August.
His buckled shoes were too large.

At the reception he hardly removed his gaze
from his goddess, Nadya of the shining hair,
shining like leaves of May. In his speech
he stuttered from John Donne's poem
The Good-Morrow: 'I wonder by my troth,
what thou and I did till we loved?'
In private, as soon as he sat down
at the table, he whispered in her ear,

in farmyard English he'd rehearsed, 'You heaven,
and we gonna live for friggin' ever.
From poetry of Ish von Barden.'
'Twang twang twang!' she said, with a hand
on her heart, as if struck
by the arrow of love's archer.
Jim stood up to make a short speech,
sat down and, amid applause, stood up again
and said, 'Why did the scarecrow win so many prizes?
... Because he was outstanding in his field'.
No laugh louder nor groan was heard in all the shire,
nor a louder clink of glasses.

And what now? – his wife being stitched,
and the sound of Goo-Gaga's crying
in the birth room, and a no-entry sign across the door.
In the pose of a clumsy contraption,
Yevich leaned against the coffee machine
and went blank.

16. Putrefaction

Putrefactio, fifth stage of decomposition, following pallor mortis, algor mortis, rigor mortis, and livor mortis; anaerobic decomposition of organic matter by bacteria and fungi that results in obnoxiously odorous things; all around the Saddleback Valley the low horizon lies like the hull of a submarine; marauders over the hills were darkening the Star of the Electric Light and Dynamo and the great reign of the supreme monarch Razórmindd.

* * *

It was months since Python's violent death,
so no wonder, even now, on such a night as this,
Yevich's mind would meander,
so disturbing was the memory. As youths,
Levi, who came to be called Python,
and Yevich and the other three brothers
spent happy seasons in the fields
and the river, and these days endured
until the time when Python got involved
with an underground sect, Bubonik RedAction Movement,
בני בליעל (*beni belial*), 'sons of uselessness'
who detest בני רשף (*beni resheph*), 'sons of the flame',
preferring to walk the snaky path of the embittered,
the untalented, the jealous, the way
and life of revenge against the world.
Yevich thought of such sects

in beat Jack Kerouac's phrase,
'Peculiarly attractive to certain shallow types'.

Something had crawled into Python's blood.
'Work,' Python said, 'is for idiots to support *me*.'
His idea of music – Python's Wolf Music was the label –
was to play nine great composers,
nine his favoured number
according to his system of reversed numerology,
at the same time, some forwards, some backwards,
and he recorded one hour of that,
then played it backwards
all over again and recorded that,
and celebrated the arhythmic results
as 'progressive', and blasted it through
the dystopia of his cottage windows.
He made a destroying chaos
out of great works of art,
slashing prints of masterpieces
and he dropped the pieces in a flutter
onto boards of glue, and such pastiches of havoc
he displayed on the outer wall of his hovel
with title captions such as *an woi thu farkin ell no*'?
and *now the orijinuls an all*,
and *sweepins ov an iyun broom*. Such productions
he proclaimed as a new revolutionary art form
that is 'for the people'. These, he said,
were a refreshing anti-spirit to unhinge
and asphyxiate and smash

those that his gangsters
called 'the ruling hegemony'.

For these projects Python won awards
and grants from the International Crime Syndicate,
international mobster agency funds
and RedAction quangos.
The spirit of Python was blowing
like a seven-headed dragon fire
across the district of Mercia and Pago Agape.
There was in him a centrifugal force
of destruction wanting to mangle everything
into a deep hole in a dark cave.

This was the threat of a diseased and plagued world,
plagued with manufactured fears,
long divorced from any covenant
of loftiness of character and spirit
into which Yevich and Nadya Romanov
would wish to bring their firstborn.
Though Python, at least, was dead.

✻

17. An ezra, a bolchek, and a ruby

In a transmigration of spirit Jessie Hypsenor displays the graciousness of a Countess under the monarch Razórmindd; excitation of atmospheric oxygen; she comes back with arms full of snow; the new spirit like glühwein stations of the soul.

* * *

'Until the night tides turn,
and comes to dark the western shore
and sparkle in the heavens all their diadems,
how beautiful that shadow flickering
with sunspots underneath the cherry tree ...'
Yevich was trying to recall a passage
from *The Epic of Ekaterinburg*,
the city in Russia, east of the Ural mountains,
with its gold-domed Church on the Blood
on the site of the 1918 Romanov executions,
as if these crimes might be covered over,
the murderers and their secret controllers
never hunted down.

He turned from the window and sat
to make a prayer for his child-thing,
if the little scaretit might be so ascribed,
that he might live for blessing and not curse,
his life a campaign for sacrifice and good,

spiritual and material cosmetics for the cosmos,
like the new Hessenberg Minor scaretit
of the neighbouring Ephanerothee Dynasty
of Gallybaggers, already restoring
the pictures of the Earth.

When the bella architetura of Jessie Hypsenor
came along the corridor of the hospital
Yevich put aside his thoughts of Python, né Levi.
Here comes Muzz *Narquoise*,
Muzz Government Bureaucracy,
Muzz Modern Fiddle-With-Phones.
'Five o'clock!' Yevich called to her.
'Mr Romanov, it's nearly six now.'
Muzz Hypsenor was still walking
as she turned her wrist to check.
'Ixnay, ixnay. Goo-Gaga Romanov.
Nadie five o'clock done baba come.'
A thousand volt charge drove into her bones.
The consciousness shut-down was over.

'Oh, oh!' Muzz Hypsenor stopped.
'Yes, I saw a star, an asterisk sign,
on the Birthing Progress Page against her name
on the computer listing. So you ...'
She walked across to Yevich
and he put out his hand,
such as it was, to shake hers,
but she placed her arms

on his shoulders and said,
'Congratulations, Mr and Mrs Romanov of that Nik!
Well *done*!' She squeezed his elbow.
It felt strangely soft.
She took his straw and twig construction
and shook hard, and said over and over
'Well done, well done, well done!
Is Mama Romanov all right?
Everything well with the scaretit?'
Yevich said, 'Beautiful, thank ... having stitches.'
Jessie Hypsenor said, 'Yes, Jenny Taylor.'
Yevich said, 'Yeah, yeah,
get that one!' and laughed with her.

Jessie Hypsenor carried on up the corridor,
scratching her hand from the straw.
Nothing was said about the morning's incident;
it was blotted out, winked at,
as Rocka Vages one time winked at
Yevich Romanov's violations committed in ignorance.
Inside a minute she came back
with jingling in her fingers.

'Look,' she said, 'Sorry about earlier ...
Only I thought ...' Yevich interrupted:
'It's alright. All have our ...
well, no, Jessie couldn't know.'

She rumbled in her bag

and held out an open hand to Yevich.
'Look. For Goo-Gaga.
Little commemoration set I've been saving
for my ... but I haven't got ...
Anyway, you must have it: a pound
from Stratford, a yeuro from Brussels,
and a smuggled old rouble from St Petersburg.
For good luck. For blessing.'
'Oh ... I ... I s-s-say!' said Yevich like a gentleman.
'Swinging ponytails! Ezra ... bolchek ... ruby.
Gifts. Marvel!'
She said, 'Ezra?'
The scarecrow man said, 'Pound.'
'Ah. So what's a *hypnograph*?'
'Well-born, noble-acting character,
high-minded. Like Bereans.'
'Ah,' she said again. 'And who's the Martyr?'
Yevich said, 'Man who came back. Big Kosmokrator.
One day appear in big sky. Big *Biiiiig* Kosmokrator.
Pull down potentates.
Ephanerothee, Greek, brought to light.
Kosmokrator *ephanerothee*. Big Big Kosmokrator.
Royal signals to mighty King.'
'Ah,' she said again, as if in a state of epiphany.
'I looked up rook and crow.
A rook's got baggy trousers and ...
Oh! Got to be back on duty a minute ago.
I'll leave you to your haruspications.'

She hurried away, callipygous and liquefactious,
looking back once with a stylish wave,
heels clicking on the linoleum floor,
the blossom of her eyes,
her hair like sands of washed gold,
each strand an ensnaring fishing line,
a thousand charming baits,
the world singing underneath its breath,
one heart softened by a new birth.

18. Trout in cling film

The hospital corridor; trout for fish oil; dual nature of the human spirit displayed in a scarecrow; pretty help; Yevich's hope for his son, and for Ephanerothee, and for his generation to hornswoggle rusting time out of more starbeating decades into the brave and bright new dazzling eon.

* * *

When he looked in his jacket
for jingling coins for a second apple juice,
the scarecrow man found four slices of tomato,
half a jay's wing,
dead earwigs
and a cut of trout wrapped in cling film
he'd slid out of the fridge that morning
into his scarecrow under-jacket.
He peeled back the cling film
and nibbled confidentially at the fish.

While he chewed on the pink trout flesh
he touched the gash
he caught that morning
on his thumb and, having forgotten
or ignored it since his lunch,
he wondered Nadya hadn't noticed.
He drooped his head and covered it with his hands,

regretting his loss of composure
at such a time of thanksgiving:
'Let, though, sea-wind of mysterious spirit
of unseen power blow it out of mind.
Hope against hope invisible stigmata
of my temper and shortcomings
will not be born in my son.'

He undid the knot
and unwrapped the handkerchief
and showed the raw wound
to the new nurse on reception duty.
Long dark hair pored around a slender pretty face.
She took Yevich to a tap and washed off
the dried and seeping ichor
and dabbed it against infection
and rolled a clean bandage
across the bleeding wound.
Cold water ran over his hand.
He smelled the scent of human hair.
'Thousands of charming baits she lays ...
Her beauteous eyes ensnare whole shoals of men ...
Each golden hair's a fishing line ...
If snow be white ...
And yet, by heaven, I think my love as rare
As any she belied with false compare.'
He thanked her and shook her hand.

The scarecrow man Isayevich 'Yevich' Ishi Romanov

sloped on a seat in the corridor,
ragged like a John the Baptist,
like bedraggled feathers of a bird in rain,
as if he'd been living off wild locusts,
the most contented man
in all the valleys of straw.

His scarecrow boondocker boots
kicked a length of chaff
out of sight, underneath the seat,
and he thought of Goo-Gaga Isayevich Ishi Romanov
in his own commission,
summers and winters, through season
into season, in heatwaves, floods
and rains, shining puddles around him,
their waters deep with stars,
his form reflected in each pool,
arms wide, hanging, on that framework
of a wooden cross
in his own shining fields of beet.

Ephanerothee-English Glossary

alektorophonia: cock-crowing (Gk., p. 14)
בני בליעל (*beni belial*): 'sons of uselessness' (Deuteronomy 13/13 et cetera, pp. 65, 72, 103)
בני רשף (*beni resheph*): 'sons of the flame' (Job 5/7: 'as sparks fly upwards, man is born for trouble'; 'sparks' is בני רשף (p. 103) (see *Keys of the Kingdom Holy Bible*)
bodging: get moving (Old Sussex, pp. 43, 77)
Brautigan: 'Gee, you're so beautiful that it's going to rain', from Richard Brautigan's poem 'Gee, you're so beautiful that it's going to rain' (p. 77)
cachexia: general physical wasting and malnutrition usually associated with chronic disease (p. 17)
cur: why (Lat., p. 70)
draves and spakes: invented implements, in mockery of 'drave' and 'spake' for 'drove' and 'spoke' (p. 101); silly curiosity in King James Bible
Ephanerothee: ἐφανερώθη (e-phan-e-rówthee), 'brought to light' (Gk., appears throughout)
ergot: fungal disease of rye and other cereals in which black elongated fruiting bodies grow in the ears of the cereal; eating contaminated food can result in ergotism (p. 15)
Gaberlunzies: beggars (Burns, p. 44)
gallyblagger: gally ('to frighten') + baggar ('beggar'); Isle of Wight, scarecrow (pp. 24, 62, 71, 85)
Geebees: KGB men (Solzhenitsyn, *The Oak and the Calf*) (p. 23)
generador del aire caliente: generator of hot air (p. 14)
haruspex es: you are a prophet (Lat., p. 70)
haruspications: a form of divination, foretelling (p. 109)
hodmedod: scarecrow (Berks., p. 24)

ichor: the fluid said to run in the veins of the gods; from YevICH + ORe (pp. 51, 112)

If snow be white ... false compare: Shakespeare, Sonnet 130 (p. 112)

indagatrix es: you are a female explorer (Lat., p. 70)

In praise of Character in the Bleak inhuman Loneliness: (Kerouac) (p. 71)

ixnay: Beat for 'no' (pp. 53, 55, 107)

Kerry: mythical Ephanerothee figure of Hellenic beauty (p. 6)

Kleptos: thieves, abbreviation of kleptomaniacs (Gk., p. 51)

Kosmokrator: κοσμοκράτωρ, world ruler (Gk., pp. 35, 41, 109)

Kupidos: cupidity, love of money (Gk., p. 51)

Oak and the Calf: memoirs of Alexander Solzhenitsyn (p. 23)

of that Nik: Play on 'of that Ilk', British aristocracy. 'Nik' is a Russian suffix: 'refusenik', 'sputnik'; also 'beatnik' (p. 6 and throughout)

pro yednu kveah tinu slunkah nesuitee: the sun does not shine for one flower only (Czech, p. 15)

Quid erat hoc?: What was this? (Lat., p. 85)

scaretit: scare + tit, little scarecrow (from friend Maggie Sawkins, winner of Ted Hughes poetry award 2014) (p. 23 and throughout)

Stakhanovite energy: In 1935 Aleksei Stakhanov, a 30 year-old miner, hewed 102 tons of coal in a six-hour shift, fourteen times his quota, hailed as a world record. To reward individual achievements in production the party launched the Stakhanovite Movement (pp. 42, 63)

Star of Remphan: from ancient Babylonian idolatry (p. 52); Bible, Acts of the Apostles, chapter 7, verse 43

sum indagatrix: I am a female explorer (Lat.), (p. 70)

tears of St Lawrence: If anybody was executed by the Romans 'meteors streaked through the night sky and reappeared every year around St Lawrence's feast day on August 10' (*The Times*, London, August 11, 2007) (p. 92)

those of Berea were more fair-minded, daily checking the Scrolls to see if things were true: Bible, Acts of the Apostles, chapter 17, verses 10-12 (pp. 94, 109)

Thousands of charming baits ... a fishing line: Edmund Waller, poem, 'Upon A Lady With An Angle' (p. 112)

Ya s'tabóy dva bérega oo adnóy rekí: You and I are the two banks of one river (Rus.) (pp. 22, 28)

Zamzummin: ancient Canaanite tribe, Bible, Deuteronomy 2/20 (page 52)

zoid: in botany, a reproductive cell that possesses one or more flagella, and is capable of independent movement; also urban slang for half mechanical and half animal (p. 14)

Zygo: yoke, union (Gk., pp. 10, 90)

Sky Music

the other side of the barbed-wire fence
along the waving field of grain
in the curving split of the horizon
between the unripe green of the cornfield
and the light blue jewellery of the splintering sky
and a few trees sparse as dried bushes
of an african wilderness
bearing no foliage even in this summer
swinging high in the sparkling waters of the clouds
this choral of a thousand mesmerizing skylarks
rhyming with nothing but the wind
battlefield angels beating oscillations
hanging poised on a tilt of wings
radiostars with meadow messages
alaudia arvensis in excelsis gloria
writing their insignia on scrolls
off-the-beat madrigals and solos
on harps of gold and horse-hair strings
uplifting vociferous larks
pre-adamite aircraft
singing in the sky
pounding at the gates
on this high hill

Afterword

'Milton! thou shouldst be living at this hour:
'England hath need of thee: she is a fen
'Of stagnant waters: altar, sword, and pen.'

So did Lakelands poet William Wordsworth write of John Milton.

Poet of Beowulf, you Chaucer, Spenser, Shakespeare, Donne, Keats, all you should be living at this late hour.

It was forty years ago I read Edmund Spenser. And so did the Honourable Roden Berkeley Wriothesley Noel (1834-1894) write of Spenser, regarding his epic *The Faerie Queene* in 16th-century Elizabethan England, published 1590 and 1596 that:–

'England was ripe and ready for a great poem ... National life was fresh, full, and young, ripe with the masterful spirit of domination, enterprise, reckless daring, and adventure; full, too, of human fault, arrogant, violent, ungovernable, sensuous, intriguing. While Italian and classical literature were as mines of treasure newly opened on earth, the translated Bible was as a burst of sunlight from among clouds of mortal corruption and tradition, blown now asunder by healthful winds in heaven ...

'The expected music broke forth twofold in the great human drama of Shakespeare, preluded by Marlowe, and in the great religio-philosophical romance of Spenser, preluded by Sidney, Sackville and his companions ... [Spenser's] stanzas I have quoted have a Dantesque grandeur of imagery ... [His effects] are often a dreamy languor and witchery of melting music, whose cadence is that of delicate wavelets on shining sand, rhythmically falling in warm summer light ... this knightly bard chanting in the early dawn' (*The Poems of Edmund Spenser, (Selected), Edited, with an Essay, Biographical and Critical, and Glossary*, published Walter Scott, London, 1887, pp. 26, 32, 33, 35).

Selection of epics and long narrative poems

Beowulf (Michael Alexander edition recommended)
Blake, William, *America, a Prophecy*
Blake, William, *A Vision of the Last Judgment*
Blake, William, *Jerusalem*
Chaucer, Geoffrey, *The Canterbury Tales*
Chaucer, Geoffrey, *The Legend of Good Women*
Coleridge, Samuel Taylor, *The Rime of the Ancient Mariner*
Cowper, William, *The Task*
Dante Alighieri, *The Divine Comedy*
Eliot, TS, *Four Quartets*
Eliot, TS, *The Waste Land*
Epic of Gilgamesh
Homer, *Odyssey* (Robert Fitzgerald edition recommended)
Homer, *The Iliad* (Robert Fitzgerald edition recommended)
Keats, John, *Endymion*
Keats, John, *Isabella, or the Pot of Basil*
Keats, John, *Lamia*
Keats, John, *The Cap and Bells*
Keats, John, *The Eve of St. Agnes*
Langland, William, *Piers Plowman*
Longfellow, Henry Wadsworth, *Hiawatha*
Longfellow, Henry Wadsworth, *Tales of a Wayside Inn*
Milton, *Paradise Lost*
Milton, John, *Paradise Regained*
Poe, Edgar Allen, *The Raven*
Pope, Alexander, *An Essay on Criticism*
Pope, Alexander, *The Rape of the Lock*
Shakespeare, William, *The Rape of Lucrece*
Shakespeare, William, *Venus and Adonis*

Shelley, PB, *Adonais*
Shelley, PB, *Epipsychidion*
Sir Gawain and the Green Knight (Bernard O'Donoghue
    edition recommended)
Spenser, Edmond, *Mother Hubberd's Tale*
Spenser, Edmond, *The Fairie Queene*
The Song of Roland
Virgil, *The Georgics*
Wordsworth, William, *Intimations of Immortality from Recollections of Early Childhood*
Wordsworth, William, *The Prelude, or Growth of a Poet's Mind*
Wordsworth, William, *Lines Composed a Few Miles above Tintern Abbey*

fly fishing only

first line of haiku
    being five-seventeenths of haiku

fly fishing only

www.ingramcontent.com/pod-product-compliance
Lightning Source LLC
Chambersburg PA
CBHW061227070526
44584CB00029B/4027